D1592081

Puppet Animation
in the Cinema

Puppet Animation in the Cinema

History and Technique

L. Bruce Holman

South Brunswick and New York: A. S. Barnes and Company
London: The Tantivy Press

A. S. Barnes and Co., Inc.
Cranbury, New Jersey 08512

The Tantivy Press
108 New Bond Street
London W1Y OQX, England

Library of Congress Cataloging in Publication Data

Holman, Loyd Bruce.
    Puppet animation in the cinema.

    Bibliography: p.
    1. Puppet films—History and criticism. 2. Puppet
films—Catalogs. I. Title.
PN1995.9.P8H6   791.43′3   73-10523
ISBN 0-498-01385-5

SBN 0-904208-60-5 (U.K)
PRINTED IN THE UNITED STATES OF AMERICA

The dream of creating a living human being by means other than natural reproduction has been a preoccupation of man from time immemorial: hence such myths as Pygmalion and Galatea. Serious mediaeval natural philosophers such as Albertus Magnus (master to Aquinas) concerned themselves with the possibility. The creation of the homunculus is a recurrent theme in literature.

—André Bazin,
"What Is Cinema?"

Contents

Preface

The animated puppet film is a form of cinema which is relatively unfamiliar to the average filmgoer in the West. In years past it was obligatory for a theatre manager to run short animated films with the showing of feature pictures—a "New Yorker" illustration from the early Thirties depicts a dejected crowd of tuxedo-ed first-nighters emerging from the *premiere* of a Hollywood extravaganza, the caption explaining their down-cast look: "No Mickey Mouse." Although Mickey has been a super-star in the U.S., relatively few fans remember George Pal's Jasper, and virtually none would recognise the names of Mr. Prokouk, Good Soldier Schweik, or Prince Bajaja. Only a few understand the puppet animation process, and fewer still are aware that this process has been used with puppets to produce hundreds of short films and a substantial number of features. Indeed, this lack of appreciation for puppet films extends beyond the casual filmgoer—film scholars in the West, even those who specialise in the study of animation, have for the most part ignored the field of puppet films. Here is a virtual galaxy of films generally unknown in the West.

It is the purpose of this work to explore the field of puppet animation, to record the history and development of the art, to describe the process of making puppet films, to suggest criteria for judging them, to describe some of the persons who have been foremost in the production of puppet films, and to compile a chronological filmography representative of the work of the world's puppet film-makers.

At present there is no single source where this information may be found. Books on animation and puppetry give only passing reference to puppet animation, each regarding animated puppets as peripheral to its field. Much of the background information for this writing has been gathered from back numbers of trade magazines, newspaper clippings, catalogues of film distributors, and pamphlets and programmes from film exhibitions. Primary sources have been interviews with persons who have produced puppet films, visitations to film studios and film archives in London, Amsterdam, Prague, Montreal, Washington, and New York, and viewings of the films themselves.

There is a sense of urgency implicit in any historical study of film. Despite the continuing efforts of a number of agencies to collect and preserve films, a large number have been lost through accident, neglect, or through decay of the film-base on which they were printed. In the case of puppet films the loss of works of historic interest is appalling. Feature films have always been considered to have some monetary and artistic value, and many have been saved by studios, archives, and private collectors; many puppet films have been less fortunate. As far as this writer has been able to determine there is no agency presently concerned with the preservation of puppet films *per se,* and it is likely that as many early puppet films are decaying in forgotten corners as are preserved in film archives. Since all art and technology is derivative to the extent that it is based on experimentation and experience of the past, it is worthwhile at least to compile a written record of as many films as possible of any category in order that the information, if not actual prints, shall be available for study by film-makers and film historians.

An additional reason for this book, and for the choice of topic, is purely personal. Puppet films at their best are a delight to experience. There is a magic in the grace and deliberation of the movement of the figures, and a quality of expression which is rarely to be found in cartoon animation or live-action films. It is hoped that the reader will share the enjoyment to be found in the works of Trnka, Starevitch, Pojar, and other masters of the puppet film.

Definitions, Clarifications and Limitations

It is difficult to draw a clear line regarding what *is* and what *is not* an animated puppet film. In general it is a film made by using free-standing, articulated puppets made of wood, plastic, or other materials. These puppets are photographed on a single frame of motion picture film, moved slightly and photographed again on the next frame of film, and so on until the action has been completed. When the finished film is projected the puppet appears to move. However, within a study of puppet animation further delineation is necessary. Most animation techniques utilise the basic principle of graduated movement photographed one frame at a time, the best-known being conventional cartoon animation in which a succession of drawings are made on paper or acetate to be photographed. Cartoon animation techniques have been described at length in a number of publications and will be considered to be outside the scope of this study except where specific references are appropriate.

Less well-known are the techniques of flat-figure and silhouette animation in which two-dimensional figures are moved and photographed on a horizontal surface. The figures are two-dimensional like those of cartoon animation, yet in method of movement and in spirit they are more closely related to puppet animation. In order to confine the study to puppet animation *per se,* these and other peripherally-related techniques will be mentioned where appropriate, but excluded from general consideration.

The definition of an animated puppet film is further complicated by the use of animated puppets as special effects devices in conventional live-action films. Consider, for example, the following judgements: *King Kong* is not an animated puppet film even though the principal character is an animated puppet. *The New Gulliver* is an animated puppet film even though the principal character is not a puppet. In the latter film the puppets are presented as surrealistic characters in a

11

surrealistic world, and the audience is not required to accept them in a human context. Ptushko, the film-maker, intended the human actor to stand out in contrast to the puppets to provide counterpoint. In *King Kong* the audience is required to suspend disbelief and accept the puppet as just what he appears to be, a giant gorilla in a human world—to view him as a puppet would destroy the whole effect of the film.

It is regrettable that only passing reference can be given here to the magnificent special effects animation of such men as Willis O'Brien, Ray Harryhausen, Jim Danforth, and George Pal, as this work is worthy of study in itself. However, for the purposes of this study we will only include those films in which the puppets are intended to be viewed as puppets, ignoring those films which employ puppets as devices to obviate the difficulties involved in obtaining live gorillas, dinosaurs, or other creatures.

In compiling the filmographies a number of difficulties and limitations have been encountered which should be known to the reader.

Short films, cartoon films, and puppet films have never had the wide publicity and distribution of feature films, and as a result many of these are extremely difficult to trace today. It has been possible for a film to be made, briefly exhibited, and then disappear, leaving behind only slight clues regarding its production and story. Wide distribution, especially in the case of puppet films in the U.S., has been rare. Often they have been exhibited only in their country of origin. This, along with the accidental loss of some films, makes the compilation of a comprehensive filmography virtually impossible. The films traced for this study, as they appear in the general filmography, are believed to form the most nearly complete index of puppet films to date. It is assumed that this listing is a representative sample of world puppet film production.

To further complicate research, when a film is distributed abroad it is frequently the practice to translate the title into the language of the various countries, or in some cases assign an altogether different name to the film. Cohl's *Le petit Faust* has been distributed as *Le petit Faust parodie*, *A Table-Top Faust*, *Little Faust*, and *Faust with Dolls*, but at least the film is recognisable by any of these titles. With some others the title in translation has no connection with the original and is in no way descriptive of the film. In this study the titles of foreign films are given in English, using either the distributor's English title or the writer's literal translation.

Assigning dates to films is sometimes a study in frustration. Theoretically the "date" of a film is its date of production (or the year in which it was completed, since some puppet films have taken several years to complete). However the dates given in film catalogues, books about films, or even on the film leader itself may reflect the production date, the copyright date, the original release date, subsequent later release dates, the date when the particular print was made, the production date as recalled in retrospect by persons connected with the film, or in some instances outright fabrications given by the distributor to "up-date" the film in the belief that new films sell better than old ones. All dates given in this study, including those in the filmography, are subject to these vagaries. If a date is listed without qualification then it is believed to be accurate, if it is prefaced *circa* (*ca.*) then there may be reason to doubt its accuracy within a year or two either way, and if the date is followed by a parenthetical question mark it may be considered to be an educated guess, based on factors known to surround the film's production.

Acknowledgements

The writer sincerely thanks the following people and organisations for their co-operation and assistance: Mr. David Allen, Dr. Marie Benešová, Mr. Jeremy Boulton, Mr. Louis Bunin, Mr. Richard Corbin, Mrs. Květa Frankenbergerová, Mr. John Halas, Miss Gillian Hartnoll, Mr. Co Hoedeman, Mr. Max Kevris, Miss Evelyn Lambart, Mr. Michel Patenaude, Mr. Břetislav Pojar, Mr. Patrick Sheen, Mr. David H. Shepard, Mr. Charles Silver, and Mr. Robert Verrall; La Bibliothèque National du Canada, Československý Filmexport, La Cinémathèque Canadienne, The Film Study Center of the Museum of Modern Art, Joop Geesink Produkties, The Motion Picture Division of the Library of Congress, The National Film Archive of the British Film Institute, and The National Film Board of Canada.

15

Puppet Animation
in the Cinema

The History of Puppet Animation

Throughout history puppets have performed to entertain and delight, and often to instruct audiences all over the world. Among the earlier artifacts found by archaeologists have been jointed figures of men and animals. It is likely that these figures were used in public presentations of stories of social or religious significance.[1] The animated film puppet has a long tradition behind him, but he himself is of a new breed. The puppets who existed before are his ancestors, but the animated puppet, who depends on the movement between frames of film to give him life, came into being after the advent of the motion picture, its use in animation, and the techniques learned from the — "trick-film."

The motion picture traces its history from optical novelties such as the phenakistiscope, the zoetrope, and the praxinoscope in the mid-Nineteenth century. These first used the phenomenon of the persistence of vision to produce the illusion of movement by the presentation of a sequence of pictures illustrating the phases of a given motion. When a picture is presented and withdrawn, the eye retains a brief after-image. When depictions of the finite steps of an action are rapidly presented in sequence, the after-image of one will blend with the image of the next and the impression of actual motion will be perceived.[2]

Optical devices using this effect were employed primarily as parlour-toys at the time of their invention, and even today with our highly sophisticated equipment it is difficult to appreciate the unique quality of the process. It is critical to an understanding of animation to recognise that our senses generally perceive time and motion in a continuous, unbroken flow. The paradox raised by Zeno ("the Eclectic," Fifth century B.C) in logically demonstrating the impossibility of the flight of an arrow because of the necessity of the arrow's remaining in a fixed location at any given moment of its flight may be seen as an equivocation resulting from the mind's inability to overrule sensory information to reconcile the concept of finite time and motion with the sense's picture of continuous time and motion. Zeno's concept was essentially cinematographic. Beyond the observation of the persistence of vision there is no experience in ordinary reality in which time and motion are fragmented and then restored.[3]

In conventional live-action motion pictures, forward time and motion are recorded as a series of finite fixed images. Projection of these images restores them to a very convincing semblance of motion. Animation, on the other hand, begins with a series of fixed images; when these are projected they come to life for the first time. The drawings or puppets used to make the images do not themselves move, and the individual frames on the film-stock are static, but because of the persistence of vision phenomenon, when the picture is on the screen Bugs Bunny and Trnka's Little Potter are as alive as Clark Gable.

The motion picture as a practical medium is the result of the efforts of many people.[4] Emile Reynaud gave public performances of hand-drawn animation on celluloid which was projected on a rear screen for audiences from 1892 to 1900. Schulze, Wedgwood, Niepce, Daguerre, Bayard, Talbot, de Saint Victor, Herschel, Archer, Maddox, and others have been given credit for inventing and perfecting the process of recording images on a photo-sensitive surface. Series of independently-posed photographs depicting motion were made by Henry Heyl. Improved photo-emulsions permitted exposure time to be reduced to the extent that sequence photography of a motion-in-progress became possible. In 1877 Eadweard Muybridge recorded the motion of a running horse on the plates of twenty-four cameras placed along the track. He continued this work, producing truly remarkable sequence-studies of animals and humans in motion. Ottomar Anschutz developed improved sequence-photography equipment and methods, and a means of projecting the photographs. Etienne-Jules Marey devised a "photographic gun" camera capable of high-speed sequence photographs. Marey, and also Hannibal Goodwin, applied photo-emulsion to transparent celluloid, permitting flexible film rather than rigid plates. And in 1888, W. Laurie Dickson, working for Thomas A. Edison, perfected a system for photographing continuous motion using perforated celluloid film, drawn through a camera with intermittent motion.[5] This has since been the basic principal of motion picture cameras.

The first "movies" consisted of short scenes of people in everyday activities, and were essentially laboratory tests of the newly-invented equipment. Soon the possibilities of using the motion picture as a public entertainment device were exploited. The success of the new medium spread rapidly, creating a demand for entertainment films. Among those which delighted early audiences were the "trick-films," in which optical effects and cinematic sleight-of-hand were used to produce magical illusions. A favourite technique involved stopping the camera in the middle of an action with the camera shutter closed, then moving the actor to a new position on the set and continuing the filming. When the film was projected the actor appeared to pop magically from one spot to another. Some of the best examples of this and other trick-film techniques can be seen in the films of Georges Méliès and the Pathé brothers. Since the basic technique of animation was known from earlier animated drawings it was a logical step to introduce the practice of exposing the film one frame at a time to produce trick-films of inanimate objects moving. In the United States James Stuart Blackton, among the first experimenters in animation, produced *The Haunted Hotel* (1907) in which furniture and objects moved by means of single-frame cinematography. In 1909 he used the same technique for *The Birth and Adventures of a Fountain Pen*.

In 1908 Arthur Melbourne Cooper, an Englishman, produced a film using live actors and trick-film techniques called *Dreams of Toyland*. Children's toys were animated to produce what may have been the earliest example of puppet animation. Cooper's *Noah's Ark,* also 1908, used similar techniques.

Emile Cohl, an early French master of the animated cartoon and trick-film, made a number of novelty films using single-frame cinematography. In *The Automatic Moving Company* (*Mobelier fidèle,* 1910) the contents of a house slide around the rooms, down the stairs and into a moving van, then out of the van and into a new house where they scuttle into their proper places. So skilfully was this done that to this day there is disagreement as to whether the sets and props were full-scale or miniatures. Shortly after this Cohl exhibited *Le petit Faust* which was made with animated puppets acting out a simplified version of the story of Faust.[6] Judging from the apparent scale of the clothing of these puppets the figures were probably six to eight inches tall. There were several sets and painted backgrounds, both interior and exterior, constructed with considerable skill. Although somewhat stiff, the movement of the figures is good considering that this was Cohl's first puppet animation. Cohl occasionally resorted to labour-saving short-cuts such as figures sliding on stage with their legs concealed behind pieces of scenery to cover the fact that their legs were not moving. In staging and presentation the film resembles the versions of stage performances which were being made in live-action pictures of the same era. Singing or spoken narration probably accompanied the original presentation of the film since a puppet chorus periodically slides on the set and stands open-mouthed while the action is temporarily halted. Off-stage voices have long been a part of puppet theatre and would have logically occurred to Cohl as a means of introducing sound into his film.

There are records of an animated toy film called *Tragedy in Toyland,* in which toy soldiers fight a duel over a doll named Miss Pru. The film was copyrighted in the United States by the Kalem company on May 17, 1911, but there is no indication of who made the film.[7]

At approximately the same time as Cohl's animation work in France, Ladislas Starevitch, then director of the Museum of Natural History at Kovno, Russia, embarked on a film study of insects. "I had to show the life of the stag beetle . . . I waited days and days to shoot a battle between two beetles, but they would not fight with the lights shining on them. So I tried trick animals [animated models]. I liked moulding them so much that I continued until I found myself making fairy-tales."[8] His insect fairy tales were popular, and in 1911 Starevitch left the museum to go to Moscow, then the centre of Russian film production. His film *The Grasshopper and the Ant* (*ca.* 1911) produced for the Hanjonkoff Society, was presented to Tsar Nicolas II and his son, and was shown in Paris at the Gaumont Palace. It is said to have been the first Russian-made film to be shown abroad.

The Revenge of a Kinographic Cameraman (*ca.* 1912) is less a fairy tale than a bedroom farce, involving the marital infidelities of Mr. Beetle (an animated model beetle) with a dragonfly. The pair are photographed through the keyhole by a jealous rival, a grasshopper who is a cameraman and projectionist. Mr. Beetle returns home to interrupt Mrs. Beetle entertaining her lover, an artist-grasshopper. Mr. Beetle drives off the artist and berates his wife for her indiscretion. Finally, they are reconciled and Mr. Beetle proposes that they forget the incident and go to the cinema. Needless to say, the feature attraction is the film of Mr. Beetle's affair with the dragonfly, and Starevitch's film ends with a three-way brawl between Mrs. Beetle, Mr. Beetle, and the Grasshopper-projectionist.

In Moscow Starevitch directed a number of live-action films based on classics and stories by Gogol and Pushkin. He found, however, that he preferred puppet animation: "Actors," he said, "always want to have their own way."[9] In 1919, following the Russian revolution, Starevitch moved to France where he continued to produce puppet films. Live actors, usually children, were often incorporated in the stories. Starevitch's daughter, Nina, played in a number of his films, including *The Voice of the Nightingale,* produced in 1923. It was

From THE TALE OF THE FOX *(1929–1939), by Ladislas Starevitch (photo courtesy of the American Film Institute).*

Ladislas Starevitch (photo reproduced from Harry Potamkin's "Ladislas Stare-vitch and His Doll Films," Theatre Guild Magazine, *Dec., 1929.).*

Scenes from Starevitch's films (Ibid.).

shown in the United States in 1925, where it received the Riesenfeld Gold Medal for the most original film of that year. Starevitch produced a great many animated puppet films in his studio in Fontenay-sous-Bois near Paris. In later years he was assisted by his daughter and collaborated with Sonika Bo. He was active in film-making until his death in 1965.

Between 1915 and 1916 Helen Smith Dayton, a New York sculptor, experimented with an animation technique which was unique at that time. Her figures were moulded from clay, and were moved and re-sculpted between exposures. Contemporary photographs showed her figures to be comic characters, about twelve inches tall, with amazing detail.[10]. Although she devoted a considerable amount of time to the project and filmed a variety of sequences, there is no record of her films being exhibited, and it is doubtful that prints exist today.

In 1917 Howard S. Moss of Chicago was operating Toyland Films,[11] producing a series of animated puppet films which were advertised as the Mo-Toy Comedies. These were distributed by the Peter Pan Film Corporation in New York as entertainment shorts for theatres.[12] At least eleven short films and one five-reel feature were made by the company, but it is not known whether prints of these exist today. Titles included *Midnight Frolic, Jimmy Gets the Pennant,* and *Out in the Rain* (all *ca.* 1917).

Willis O'Brien might be called the Dean of American special effects animators, his credits in live-action pictures including the animation in *The Lost World, King Kong,* and *Mighty Joe Young.* It is not generally known that he produced animated puppet films before going into special effects work. Using naturalistic puppet figures he made three comedies set in prehistoric times: *The Dinosaur and the Missing Link, R.F.D. 10,000 B.C.,* and *Prehistoric Poultry; The Dinornis or the Great Roaring Whiffenpoof* (all copyrighted in 1917). The stories were like those of contemporary silent comedies with an abundance of slapstick and brutality-humour. The animation of the puppets flows well, particularly in the portions of stage-business which O'Brien devised: a caveman puppet walks into a low-hanging tree limb and falls backward, seeing stars; he rises, and looking back at the offending limb, walks into another. O'Brien seems particularly adept in animating the prehistoric animals in his films. His next effort was a sample-film called *The Creation,* a short vignette showing a live actor hunting animated prehistoric animals, which was made as a prospectus to interest producers in backing a special effects feature. His three puppet films were produced by Conquest Pictures and distributed by Thomas A. Edison, Inc.

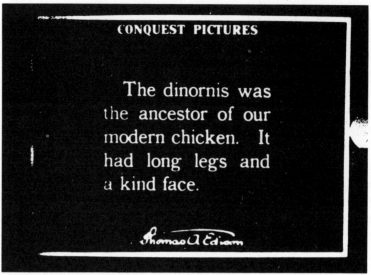

A title-card from PREHISTORIC POULTRY (1917), by Willis O'Brien (photo by L. Bruce Holman).

Edwin Miles Fadman, working in the United States, created puppet films during the Twenties. His works, which were produced by the Red Seal Company and distributed by the Pathé Exchange, included *Mose and Funny Face Make Angel Cake* (1924) and *Cracked Ice* (*ca.* 1924, copyrighted 1927).

During the late Twenties in the U.S.S.R. Alexandr Ptushko, a cartoonist, turned to puppet film making. He produced several short films, including *The Bed Bug* and *Play and Work* (1930 or earlier). Forming a collective with a number of other artists and technicians he produced a series of tales involving the antics of a puppet character called "Bratishkin." Having mastered the techniques of puppet animation for story-telling, Ptushko and the other members of the collective began what was to be three years of work to produce a feature-length film based on Swift's "Gulliver's Travels." The script, written by Ptushko and G. Roshal was drawn from Gulliver's adventures in the land of the Lilliputians, and was a political satire of monarchy and a glorification of the workers who arise to overthrow it. The story of *The New Gulliver* begins at a Pioneer camp: While one of the camp leaders is reading "Gulliver's Travels" to a group of children, Petya, the hero of the film (played by V. Konstantinov), falls asleep. He "awakes" to find himself in Lilliput, tied to the ground with string and surrounded by an army of puppets. Because of the skilful planning of the shots of the "real" Petya and mechanically-moved puppets, and a life-sized model of Petya and the animated puppets, the impression is given that Petya and the puppets are freely interacting. The film follows Swift's story but the characterisations of Ptushko are far more satirical than those of Swift. The Prime Minister is incredibly Machiavellian, and the King is depicted as a simpering idiot whose speeches come from a gramophone concealed beneath his robe. Petya becomes disgusted with the nobility, and suspicious of the large army and police force; soon he discovers that beneath the city there are factories and mines where the workers are held in bondage. Petya joins the workers in their plan to revolt. A great battle ensues, and with Petya's help the workers are victorious. Petya awakes to find himself still at the Pioneer camp with the other children teasing him for falling asleep during the reading of the story.

The New Gulliver was the most elaborate puppet film undertaken to that time. It was shown at Cannes in 1934 (a year before it was to be released) where it received acclaim for its artistry and technique. In 1939 Ptushko produced *The Little Golden Key,* a short puppet film. Later he went into special effects work and directed live-action works.

George Pal, who is better known today as a producer and director of live-action films usually involving elaborate and skilful special effects, was for twenty years the leading puppet animator of England and the United States. Born in Cegléd, Hungary, Pal began his film career at the Huwia studio in Budapest. Later he worked as an art designer for UFA Studios in Berlin. His earliest remaining animated film is *Midnight,* an advertisement for a Berlin cigarette company. In 1933 Pal went to Eindhoven, Holland, where he produced animated puppet films for Philips Radio in a studio provided by the company. Among these works were *Ether Ship* and *The Magic Atlas.* Pal's puppets were made of wood, with flexible arms and legs. The heads were removable so that changes of expression could be achieved by simply interchanging one head for another. The characters resembled turned wooden toys, and the style which Pal established can still be seen in the puppet films produced for Philips today.

In about 1935 Pal went to London, where he produced three puppet films for Horlick's Malted Milk: *On Parade* (1936), *What Ho, She Bumps!* (1937), and *Sky Pirates* (1937). He also produced a series of films based on "The Thousand and One Nights": *Ali Baba, Sinbad,* and *Aladdin and the Wonderful Lamp* (ca. 1936). Pal arrived in the United States in 1940 to produce the Puppetoon series of theatrical shorts for Paramount Studio. The Puppetoons played primarily in Paramount theatres from 1940 to 1949, and are virtually the only animated puppet films which have been seen by large audi-

Wooden puppets from George Pal's ON PARADE (photos reproduced from World Film News, *August, 1937).*

ences in the U.S.A. These films have been withdrawn from circulation and are unlikely to be re-released in theatres, considering the current decline in the screening of "cartoons" with feature films. Particularly unlikely for re-release, in light of the contemporary racial situation in the United States, is Pal's *Jasper* series, in which a puppet represents a stereotype Negro boy comedy figure. In 1950 Pal turned to special-effects animation, creating the animated model rockets in *Destination Moon,* for which he received an Academy Award. He has received this award on three subsequent films, in addition to the special Academy

Award for animation which was presented for the puppet film *John Henry* (1946).

After George Pal left for England, work in the studio in Holland was assumed by one of Pal's associates, Joop Geesink.[13] Joop Geesink and his brother Wim continue to make commercial films for Philips and other clients, as well as entertainment shorts. Making a pun on their use of animated puppets they dubbed the studio "Dollywood." Under their direction Dollywood produced animated puppet films for the commercial market. Today, as Joop Geesink Produkties in Amsterdam, the studio is the major producer of puppet and object animation for advertising and public-information films for cinemas and television, with clients in Europe and the United States. Philips continues to be a major client for the studio, and has commissioned several animated puppet shorts, the more recent of which were directed by Max Kevris. These include: *The Travelling Tune* (1960), using three-dimensional paper puppets telling the story of a French composer's tune which passes from one country to another until it circles the globe and returns to Paris; *Philips Cavalcade: 75 Years of Music* (1964), a brief synopsis of the history of music from classical to rock, made with puppet caricatures of personalities from the world of music and art; and *Philips on Parade* (1967) in which the Philips Marching Band

Property storage at the Joop Geesink studio (photo by the writer).

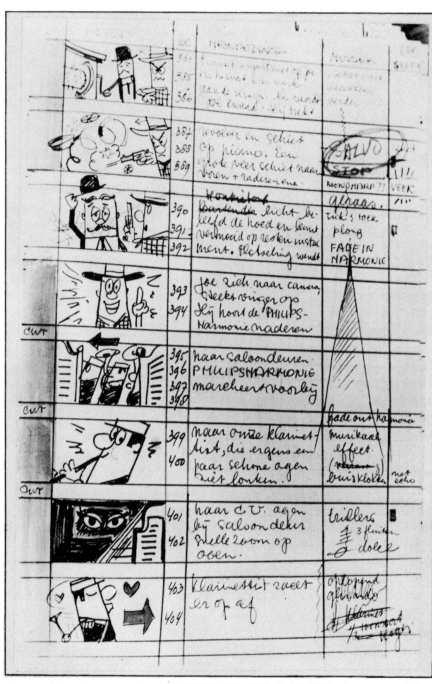

A page from the story-board of PHILIPS ON PARADE (courtesy of Joop Geesink Produkties).

(about thirty wooden puppets) marches around the world bringing cheer and Philips products to people of other lands.

The Geesink company has expanded operations, moving its studios into new quarters with multiple animation and design areas, and complete workshop facilities for the production of puppets, sets, and stage properties. Additionally, the company has formed Starfilm, a division for the production of live-action films.

Len Lye, who is known for his films from the Thirties using multiple-printing and filters to achieve effects which are only today being re-discovered by makers of "psychedelic" films (*Colour Box, Rainbow Dance, Doing the Lambeth Walk,* and *Trade Tattoo*), also made two animated puppet films. The first, referred to as *"Experimental Animation"* was made in Great Britain in 1933. Presumably it was intended as no more than an experiment in animation technique— the action consists of a monkey and a dancing palm tree singing "Peanuts." The second was a commercial film for Shell Oil, *Birth of a Robot,* which he made with Humphrey Jennings in 1936. The animation and use of colour in the film are excellent, but it is assumed that some degree of tongue-in-cheek humour was intended by Lye in using a narrator whose voice sounds suspiciously like Westbrook van Vorheese narrating *The March of Time* series. The ponderous voice narrates the story of an explorer and his car who are lost in the desert; their only hope for survival is a service station which turns out to be a mirage. They perish, but Venus, looking down from a celestial party, takes pity and sends down drops of oil which fall on the bleached bones of the explorer. He is reborn as The Robot (Shell's logo at that time), and marches out to keep the wheels of industry turning.

In Germany the Diehl brothers produced a number of short puppet films and several full-length features. Two of their major productions were *Puss in Boots (ca.* 1936) and *The Seven Ravens* (1937). The puppets of the Diehls were extremely naturalistic, perhaps the most life-like which have been made. The figures had finely-moulded features with movable mouths; the skin of the faces and hands appears to be rubber. Costumes and sets were elaborate, with an abundance of detail. Of particular note is a scene from *Puss in Boots* in which Puss plots to trick an evil magician who waits to trap the king and Puss's master. Puss feigns ignorance of the magician's abilities and asks for a demonstration. The vain magician transforms himself into an elephant, a lion, and then into a mouse—at which point Puss pounces and eats him. The handling of the puppets in this sequence is virtually flawless. The general impression is that one is watching a live actor and real animals rather than puppets. However, elsewhere in the film one becomes aware that it is impossible to duplicate every nuance in human actions. The contrast of extreme naturalism in the puppets with their occasional stilted movements is distracting for the viewer.

In France Jean Painlevé and René Bertrand recounted the story of Bluebeard in *Barbe-Bleue* (1938) using nearly three hundred puppets made of plasticine clay. The film, which was shot in colour, was quite elaborate, and undoubtedly painstaking to produce. Ralph Stephenson describes the film as macabre and ironic.[14]

Among those who saw Ptushko's *The New Gulliver* were Karel Dodal, a Czechoslovak cartoon animator, and his former wife, Hermína Týrlová. While married to Dodal, Týrlová had worked with him making animated cartoon films, and they decided to collaborate on a combined puppet and cartoon film, *The Adventures of Mr. Pry* (1936). In 1938 they worked together again to produce a puppet film, *The Lantern Mystery,* an advertisement for the Krasá Footwear Company. When the Nazis entered Czechoslovakia, Dodal was forced to emigrate, and Týrlová was left alone. However, being a woman of exceedingly strong character (her early life had been a succession of tragedies), Týrlová was determined not to give up film-making. She purchased a second-hand camera and began making a film from Ondřej

Hermína Týrlová with Ferda the Ant (photo ca. 1942, reproduced from František Tenčík's Hermína Týrlová).

Scenes from Diehl brother's PUSS IN BOOTS (frame-enlargements by the writer).

Sekora's book "Ferda the Ant." *Ferda the Ant* was completed in 1942, after Týrlová had taught herself the techniques of puppet construction, single-frame animation, camera operation, and had obtained financial backing from the Zlín Studio. For four years this was occupied by the Nazis, and Týrlová was able to do only minor technical work there. Following the liberation of Czechoslovakia in 1945, Týrlová completed an anti-Nazi, anti-war film, *The Revolt of the Toys*. At seventy years of age Hermína Týrlová is the First Lady of animated puppet films. Most of the nearly forty works she has produced can be enjoyed by adults, but are intended specifically for children. " . . . I am as happy when I succeed with films as another woman when she knits a pretty jumper for her child. I knit my films to please children . . . I have no family and my creative work replaces it. Maybe that is why I am not unhappy, or embittered like lonely women usually are."[15]

In 1946 Louis Bunin created a series of animated puppets caricaturing Hollywood celebrities as a prologue to M-G-M's musical feature *The Ziegfeld Follies*. Among those depicted were Will Rogers, W. C. Fields, Eddie Cantor, and Fanny Brice. *Alice in Wonderland,* released in 1951, was a feature-length version of Lewis Carroll's story, using Bunin's puppets with a live actress playing Alice. The film has been compared to Walt Disney's cartoon film of Alice, to Disney's disadvantage.[16] Bunin's short animated films include *'Homer, the Horse Who Couldn't Talk* (1958), created for the Brussels World Fair, and *The Dingo Dog and the Kangaroo* (1969). Bunin has also been one of the most prolific creators of television commercials in the United States using animated puppets. He designed and animated the *Mr. Lookit* logo for CBS, and produced more than sixty commercials for Utica Club Beer using "Schultz and Dooley," a pair of animated beer mugs. In all, he has produced over five hundred commercials and television inserts using puppets, flat-figure, and a variety of other animation techniques.

While Hermína Týrlová worked at Gottwaldov, another group of Czechoslovak film artists established a puppet film studio in the mediaeval section of Prague. Their director was a man who was to become the greatest master of the animated puppet film, Jiří Trnka.

Trnka was born in 1912 in Plzeň (then in Bohemia), his father a plumber, his mother a dress-maker. His early interest in art and puppetry was encouraged by his mother and by his teachers, who included Josef Skupa who later became one of the leading figures in Czech puppet theatre. Trnka attended the School of Applied Arts, and supported himself by designing puppets for Skupa's Holiday

Jiří Trnka (Česk. Filmexport).

Camp puppet theatre and drawing illustrations for books and magazines. Following his graduation at twenty-three, Trnka established his own puppet theatre. The troupe fared well in Plzěn, and a year later moved to Prague, but in the capital they were not able to attract a sufficient audience, and soon the theatre was forced to close. During the war Trnka illustrated children's books, painted, and designed sets and costumes for the stage. Following the liberation, Trnka joined a group of artists who had formed a film animation group calling themselves the Trick Brothers Studio. Trnka's first film, which had originally been scripted for puppets, was made in cartoon animation. Trnka's soft watercolour style, developed for book illustrations, was used to advantage in *Grandpa Planted a Beet*—one of the first cartoon films to break away from the "comic book" style of the Walt Disney studios. With Trick Brothers Trnka made three more cartoon films: *The Animals and the Brigands,* which won an award for Best Cartoon Film at the Cannes Festival in 1946; *The Gift,* a film satirising bourgeois society; and *The Chimney Sweep,* a classic anti-Nazi film. Despite his success, however, at illustration and at cartoon film directing, Trnka's first love was still in puppetry. In 1946, aged thirty-four, he left the cartoon studio, and with some of his fellow animators established a puppet film studio. Their first work was a short episode called *Bethlehem,* which later became the last section of the film *The Czech Year* (1947). *The Czech Year* and some of the individual

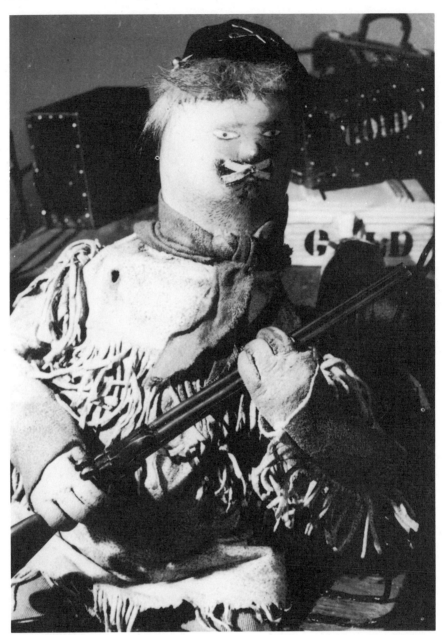

SONG OF THE PRAIRIE (1949), by Jiří Trnka. This figure, the stage-coach guard, is assumed to be a self-caricature of Trnka (photo courtesy of Ceskoslovenský Filmexport).

Two stagecoach horses from SONG OF THE PRAIRIE (photo courtesy of Ceskoslovenský Filmexport).

episodes from it won a number of international prizes, and established Trnka and his fellow-workers as the leaders of puppet film-making in the world.

Trnka's career could be drawn as an ascending spiral: he alternately produced films, turned back to design and illustration, and then refreshed, returned to puppet film production, each time topping his previous accomplishments. A true genius, and often the centre of artistic controversy, Trnka's contributions to puppet film making are many. He provided the world with the most artistic, poetic, and delightful puppet films which have been made. He set standards for artistry and quality which forced all other puppet film-makers to evaluate their work in the light of that produced in the Prague studio. And, using a production-team method of working, he trained other puppet film-makers who worked with him.[17]

Trnka directed fourteen puppet films and designed for several others which were produced in the Prague studio. Outstanding among his works are *The Czech Year* (1947), *The Devil's Mill* (1951), *Old Czech Legends* (1953), the feature-length *A Midsummer Night's Dream* (1959), and his last film, which has been called the epitome of puppet films, *The Hand* (1965). Always of a strong will and free spirit, Trnka was among the Czechoslovak artists and writers who voiced opposition to the Soviet domination of their country, and *The*

Puppet figures by Bretislav Pojar (photo courtesy of Ceskoslovenský Filmexport).

More puppets created by Bretislav Pojar (photo courtesy of Ceskoslovenský Filmexport).

Hand has been interpreted as a grim allegory of Czechoslovakia's situation.[18]

An animator who was with Trnka from the beginning of the puppet film studio in Prague is Břetislav Pojar. Pojar worked beside Trnka in making *Bethlehem:* " . . . we knew about cartoon animation, but we had to teach ourselves how to animate puppets . . . Trnka and the rest of us learned together."[19] Pojar produced *The Gingerbread Cottage* (1951) using puppets designed by Trnka, and had Trnka's assistance in making *A Drop Too Much* (1954), which was awarded a Grand Prix at Cannes. He has since produced a number of films in a variety of animation techniques including paper, flat-figure, and cartoon animation, and also a live-action feature for children, *The Gold Bay Adventure* (1954). He has worked at the National Film Board of Canada making *To See or Not to See* (1968) and is presently in Prague where he has been at work on a series of films using animated teddy bears. While Pojar learned much in Trnka's studio, his style today is uniquely his own. His imaginative and innovative work, particularly in the animation of puppets on glass, as in *It's Hard to Recognise a Princess* (1968), have earned him a place as one of the leading animators in the world.

Others who trained in the Czechoslovak studios are V. Zykmund and A. Vesela, whose films include *Budulinek and the Foxes, Night in the Picture Gallery,* and *The Goat and the Hedgehog,* and Miloš Makovec who produced *The Lost Sentry.* Stanislav Latal, who assisted with the production of *The Hand,* is presently a director at the Prague studio.

Karel Zeman, a Czechoslovak director who works from the Gottwaldov studio, has been called the heir to Georges Méliès.[20] His use of trick-film techniques equals and often surpasses the most ambitious of Méliès's. However, he began in puppet animation, working with Hermína Týrlová, and he draws upon the techniques learned in the puppet studio for his incredible trick-film and special effects work. His first picture was *A Christmas Dream* (1946), a puppet film using an animated rag-doll figure. At the Cannes Festival it received acclaim as the Best Children's Film at the same time that Trnka's *Animals and the Brigands* was awarded the prize for *Best Cartoon Film.* Following this Zeman directed a series of puppet films using an amusing little Everyman, *Mr. Prokouk,* who lampooned hoarding, superstition, bureaucracy and inventions which do not work. His film *Inspiration* (1949) deserved its title—a tribute to Czech glass-workers, the film uses animated glass figurines to tell the love story of Pierrot and Columbine. The story begins and ends in a drop of water. Zeman

Karel Zeman (Česk. Filmexport).

was able to impart movement and grace into the tiny glass figures, and tell a story which still touches and delights audiences wherever it is shown. *King Lavra* (1950), Zeman's next puppet film, was a variation of the story of King Midas. Then came *The Treasure of Bird Island* (1952), a puppet film with figures and sets designed after Persian miniature paintings. With *Journey into Prehistory* (1955) Zeman began using trick-film techniques in live-action pictures—four boys journey by boat through a land of animated dinosaurs and other creatures. *An Invention for Destruction* (1958) and *Baron Munchhausen* (1961) further developed his style—he was now combining live actors with models, animated figures, enlargements of old engravings, and a host of trick-film techniques.

Zeman continues to enlarge upon his repertory. *The Jester's Tale* (1964), and *The Stolen Airship* (1967) both use elaborate special effects. The former has been regarded as a perceptive anti-war satire featuring two musketeers during the Thirty-Years' War; the latter an adventure story based on Jules Verne's "Mysterious Island."

In Poland puppet films are produced principally at the Miniature Film Studio in Warsaw (SE-MA-FOR) and at the Puppet Film Studio at Tuszyn, near Łódź, both divisions of Film Polski, the state-owned film industry. Since the end of the Second World War Poland has been one of the largest producers of animated puppet films. While their animators are less well-known than those of Czechoslovakia the total number of films produced in the Polish studios may well exceed those of the Czechoslovak studios.

Zenon Wasilewski was the earliest Polish puppet animator. Wasilewski's first production was *The Dragon of Kraków* (1946), followed by *The Times of King Krakus* (1947). Later films include *The Bad Little Fox* (1951), *The Crime on Cat-the-Ventriloquist Street* (1962), and *The Wooden Horseman* (1965). Włodzimierz Haupe and his wife Halina Bielińska have directed puppet films separately and as a team. Haupe's first puppet film was *The Rascal Snail* (1951), and together they made *What the Moon Saw* (1955), from a story by Hans Christian Andersen about a small boy during the French revolution. *The Barrel-Organ* (1956) is from a tale by Bolesław Prus, in which a fussy middle-aged man who likes only classical music comes to realise, through the blindness of a neighbour's child, that the barrel-organ which plays in the streets is a delight for children. Teresa Badzian is a prolific puppet animator who trained as an assistant to Haupe and Bielińska. Her films, like those of Hermína Týrlová, are intended for children, and often use toys and rag dolls

A scene from Zeman's INVENTION FOR DESTRUCTION (Česk. Filmexport).

Włodzimierz Haupe at work on THE BARREL-ORGAN (photo reproduced from Cyril Beaumont's Puppets and Puppetry*).*

as puppets. Among the many films which she has directed are *The Strange Voyage* (1955), *Little Music* (1962), and *The Little Kangaroo* (1967). One of Wasilewski's early assistants was Edward Sturlis, whose films include *The Boastful Knight* (1955) in which a braggart knight, resembling Don Quixote, sallies against the Saracens. Sturlis's puppets are cleverly designed and well-animated, and his films exhibit a continuous refinement of technique. His films have been criticised for unimaginative scripting,[21] but through the Sixties his work has reflected a growing concern for social issues. It must be remembered that in Soviet-monitored countries film directors do not always have as great a latitude for selection of stories as do those in the West.

In East Germany Katja Georgi, wife of film director Klaus Georgi, has been making puppet films since 1959. Formerly a cartoon film artist her first puppet film was *The Princess and the Pea*. She works at the DEFA (State Film Organisation) studio in Dresden, and has recently completed *Der Gardinentraum (Curtain-Dream)*. Also with DEFA are Günter Rätz, Johannes Hempel, Kurt Weiler, Hans Ulrich Wiemer, Kurt Herbert Schulz, and Jörg D'Bombá. Rätz has used animated stuffed toys to produce a series of fairy and morality tales. He has made about twenty puppet films since 1958, including *Teddy Brumm* (1958), *Song of the Dove* (1960), and *Stamp Collecting* (1968). Hempel's films include *Jorinde and Joringel*, *The Little Hare and the Well*, and *Tales and Yarns*. Weiler has directed *The Story of the Five Brothers*, *The Stolen Nose*, and *The Secret Path*. Wiemer's work includes *The Street Is Not a Playground*, a safety film for children, and *Adventures in Space*. Schulz has made *The Magic Cask* and *The Wonder-Working Doctor*. Jörg D'Bombá is better known for his cartoon animation, but has also produced puppet films. *We Build a School* (1961) and *Robber Baron in the Country* are two of his puppet productions.

In Canada Alma Duncan directed several puppet films for the National Film Board. *Folksong Fantasy* (*ca.* 1956) was the first. The quality varies through the several sequences, but on the whole the film is a creditable effort. The animated birds in the "Who Killed Cock Robin" sequence are particularly well-designed, and the lighting and staging are effectively dramatic. *Kumac the Sleepy Hunter* (1958) is based on an Eskimo legend about an Eskimo who is unable to gain a wife because he is too sleepy to hunt seals. One day he rescues a sea-god whose kayak has overturned and is rewarded by being given the ability to catch more seals than anyone. He soon finds a wife and fills their igloo with seals, but when he tells her about the sea-god's gift the spell is broken and he returns to his old sleepy self. The design of the puppets, costumes, and sets is excellent. Multiple heads were used for changes of expression, and the design of the faces is very appealing. The animation of the figures is somewhat stiff, but the pacing of the film is rapid enough for this to be seldom distracting. *One Little Indian* (*ca.* 1960) is a film for children which tells of a magical Indian boy who comes to the city with a Wild West show. As he travels about the city he (and the children in the audience) learns the rules of traffic safety. Several of the puppet characters from the film are particularly imaginative: the Indian boy, the penguin man, and the vain magic moose. Although the film appears somewhat dated in style it is still popular in Canada and the United States.

Evelyn Lambart, who worked on the production of these films, is known as Norman McLaren's principal assistant. She is presently exploring unique applications of flat-figure animation in *The Horder* and a one-minute television spot dealing with forest fire safety.

Within the past few years animated puppet films with a high quality of design and camera-work have been produced by studios in Japan. This is not surprising considering that country's past tradition of patient craftsmanship and its rapidly growing technical capacity. The Gakkin Studio in Tokyo has produced a number of films which exhibit a high degree of skill in set-design, lighting, colour, and camera-work. Their films include *The Rolling Rice Ball, The Man Who Wanted to Fly,* and *The Crane's Magic Gift.* Characterisations and plot situations are well-presented, with skilful portrayal of humour and pathos. The puppets are of the Czech type and, although not equal in character and design to the best of the Czechoslovaks, are skilfully handled and have undeniable charm. Folk-tales using animals and human characters have been the dominant themes.

Co Hoedeman, a young animator from Holland, has studied at the film studios in Czechoslovakia and is presently working with the National Film Board of Canada. Hoedeman has completed *Odd Ball* (1968) and *Matrioska* (1969), and is at work on a series of Eskimo tales using animated puppets modelled after the figures of Eskimo artists. *Odd Ball* uses a figure made of white plastic-covered wire which interacts with an assortment of balls of varying sizes and colours—the degree of control of the figure and the grace which Hoedeman has imparted it may remind the viewer of Chaplin's

Co Hoedeman at the National Film Board of Canada (photo by L. Bruce Holman).

"balloon dance" from *The Great Dictator. Matrioska* uses a set of "nesting dolls" (each is hollow, and when opened reveals another smaller doll inside); the film may also be seen as Chaplinesque in that a seemingly endless series of entertaining combinations is carried out using a simple set of props.

David W. Allen, in the United States, began in animation by designing and constructing creatures for amateur films, such as Mark McGee's *The Equinox* (1965). His work in figure animation is outstanding, and he has since produced an animated puppet film *The Selfish Giant* (*ca.* 1969) from a story by Oscar Wilde. Allen's puppets use metal armatures (frequently stainless steel) with cast rubber and plastic bodies. The craftsmanship of his figures is excellent—perhaps the best construction of puppets being done today. He is presently with Cascade Pictures where he has done commercials for Nestlé's Chocolate, and animated Poppin' Fresh, the Pillsbury Doughboy. Additionally Allen contributed animation to the British production *When Dinosaurs Ruled the Earth* (1971).

Puppet armatures by David Allen (photo by David Allen).

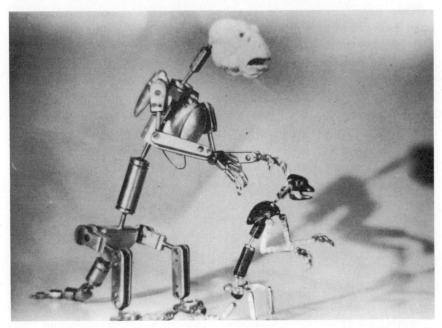

What direction is puppet animation likely to take in the future? It would seem that conventional applications of puppet animation techniques have been thoroughly explored. Films for children, entertainment films, and serious stories have been perfected by the past masters of the art. Where is the challenge for the new film artist who wishes to use puppet techniques?

Puppet films will continue to be produced, but unlike the past, are more likely to be regarded as serious art than entertainment. As Marshall McLuhan has pointed out, television has made the motion picture an obsolescent technology, and the obsolescence of a technology frees that technology from the burdens of its utilitarian applications and permits it to be employed as an art form.[22] The cinema, no longer being the primary means of mass entertainment, has become a major art form during the latter half of this century. The "Hollywood factory" system of producing extravagant films for huge profits is rapidly dying. The film director is today regarded as an artist rather than a foreman, and it is expected that his films will reflect his individual approach to contemporary social issues and will meet contemporary aesthetic standards. This change can be seen in the short film as well as in features. Mickey Mouse and Donald Duck are gone; their films are still screened from time to time but there are no new ones being made. With the passing of Walt Disney the "mouse factory" will never be the same. Today new animators, from countries which were never before known for their cartoon films, are producing works of startling originality.

Piotre Kamler, an animator/artist from France, has said, "Why take pains to animate a flower if the wind does it without any trouble at all? Perhaps in order to allow the flower to act in a way it would not otherwise do: become a bird, recite a poem of Apollinaire, or simply disappear. Or resemble no other flower in existence, while still remaining a flower animated by the wind."[23] Kamler's *The Spiderelephant* (1968) is a striking film which uses cartoon animation techniques in an altogether original fashion. Strange creatures move through a fantasy world, and yet behave with a logic which makes sense in their context. The viewer is drawn into this world and caught up in the actions of these strange beings, and perhaps learns something of himself in learning to understand these creatures.

From Japan Yoji Kuri creates a nightmare world in which amorphous cartoon characters perform acts of humour, sadism, and sexuality. Ryan Larkin of Canada uses ink-blobs to illustrate the various gaits of people in *Walking* (1969). Jan Svankmajer uses live actors in gigantic puppet-costumes in *Messrs. Schwarzwalde and*

Edgar's Last Trick and hand-puppets and collage in *The Coffin Factory,* to establish a new style of film in Czechoslovakia.

As the forms of animated films change so do their themes. Today's art is shaped by today's thought. It is unlikely that an innovative puppet animator will choose to re-tell well-known fairy-tales to produce entertainment films. Instead, it is probable that the work of the new animator will reflect his stance as an artist commenting upon social or philosophical issues.

Some recent puppet films suggest probable directions which the field may take in the future. While the animation employs the same technical principles of earlier films, their images resemble little which has preceded them. It is to be expected that the work of puppet animators who are exploring the outer limits of the art should produce films which appear strange in comparison to the works of their predecessors. Co Hoedeman's *Odd Ball* is a charming and appealing film, but it definitely is odd. The white wire figure which is used in the film bears only slight resemblance to the puppets of the "classical" style, and any number of messages can be read into the simple story of the figure who plays with a succession of strange coloured balls and eventually flies away on one. It would not be unreasonable to interpret *Odd Ball* as a study of psychedelic drug exploration, or the story might be seen as representing the protagonist's difficulties in selecting from the alternatives offered in a complex world. Hoedeman, although not being deliberately enigmatic, prefers to leave the interpretation to the viewer. Jerzy Kotowski in Poland uses a wide variety of techniques ranging from traditional puppets in *The Musical Box,* to wire figures in *The World in Opera,* and animated skeleton hands in *Shadow of Time.* Stefan Schabenbeck, also Polish, has used paper and cartoon animation, and has invented new applications for existing equipment. His puppet film *Stairs* (1969), produced in black-and-white and CinemaScope, depicts a small human figure struggling to climb a stairway in a world which is all stairs, and can be interpreted as a commentary on the contemporary human condition.

Parallel with the development of new forms there is likely to be a continuation of traditional puppet films as well. Many of the masters of the art are still at work producing entertainment and dramatic films. Established studios do not as a rule change their styles rapidly. However, considering the shifting aesthetic and philosophical mood of the times and the change of cinema-audiences from middle-aged, middle-class viewers to a younger more highly-educated set, it is predictable that new styles and new themes will become the more accepted form. The experimental animated films which are now shown primarily at film festivals and in cinema society screenings are beginning to move into the commercial cinema. Audiences will see many arresting and thought-provoking films. New artists with new concerns entering a field which has sixty years of past tradition and experience on which to build should result in a vital blend. Following the evolution of the animated puppet film through the next few years should prove a most interesting experience.

A puppet by B. Pojar for THE LION AND THE SONG (Česk. Filmexport).

The Technique
of Puppet Animation

PRODUCTION

How does one undertake producing a puppet film? Basically the process is simple: A movable puppet is constructed and placed before a motion picture camera which is equipped with a single-frame exposure device which permits the frames of film to be advanced and exposed individually, one frame at a time rather than continuously. The puppet is photographed on a single frame of film, then moved to the next position required for the motion which he is enacting, and photographed on the next frame of film. This process is repeated until the desired motion is completed.

However, like many seemingly simple processes there are innumerable possible complications. The first of these is the number of movements required to produce relatively smooth motion. As the standard projection speed of sound film is twenty-four frames per second, theoretically the puppet must be moved and photographed twenty-four times for each second of finished film—in other words, one thousand four hundred and forty movements and photographs for each minute of screen time. In practice this number is sometimes reduced by photographing the puppet twice in each stage of movement and correspondingly increasing the distance which it moves. This is referred to as "shooting on two's." The number of movements is decreased to seven hundred and twenty per screen minute. Increasing the number of shots per movement is risky; while the audience can interpolate motion from a series of rather widely-spaced positions, the persistence of vision phenomenon ceases to operate below ten or twelve images per second, and the picture becomes jerky and exceedingly annoying to watch.

The problem of how far to move a puppet or its arm or leg between shots is difficult. If the movements are too large, the action will appear to jump and will be too rapid; if they are too small, the action will be smooth but perhaps too languid for the desired effect, and more complicated to film. Timing normal human action is some help as a reference,[24] but a puppet's gestures are not those of a human. The puppet's gestures are somewhat like those of the mime—highly stylised to convey specific effects.

While it is not possible to formalise every movement which a puppet makes to arrive at universal formulas, the puppet animator can devise methods of operation to assist him. For example, if a puppet is to cross from one part of the set to another the animator may pick up the puppet and move it across the distance, judge whether the rate of speed is suitable for the desired effect, and time the movement with a stop-watch (he might also use his hand as a stand-in for the puppet, or simply make the movement in his mind's eye). Having established the time required for the movement in seconds, he then multiplies by twenty-four to establish the number of frames of film which will be exposed during the movement. He then measures the distance to be covered during the movement. Having previously measured the gait of the puppet to determine the average distance covered by the puppet's stride, the animator divides this distance into the distance to be covered during the movement. He then divides the number of steps into the number of frames of film to establish how many portions of movement and exposures are necessary for each step. This naturally pre-supposes that the rate of movement is constant; if it is not, then the calculation must be performed for each part of the movement. In actual practice the experienced puppet animator does not perform these calculations for every movement. He is familiar with the results of his work, and knows what effects are predictable from given rates of movement and how many frames of film should be allotted for specific actions. In the craft of puppet animation experience is the most reliable guide. The subtlety of movement and expression achieved by masters like Ladislas Stare-vitch and Jiří Trnka are remarkable examples of how the mechanical limitations of the medium can be overcome or turned to advantage.

The cartoon animator has one great advantage over the puppet animator: since the action in cartoon animation is accomplished by photographing a sequence of drawings, the animator has only to refer to these drawings and his "dope-sheet" (animation plotting sheet) to determine where his figures have come from, where they are going, and what the intervening action is. The animated puppet, like the arrow in Zeno's paradox, can be seen only in the position which he is occupying at any given moment. The puppet animator

Miloš Makovec filming THE LOST SENTRY (Česk. Filmexport).

may refer to notes, script, or story-board to help keep track of a puppet's actions, but at the time of filming the puppet's previous movements exist only in the animator's memory and as an invisible latent image on the film. This isolation-in-time can be turned to advantage by the skilful puppet animator. Since movement is not rigidly fixed, as in the cartoon animator's completed sequence of drawings, there is some latitude for spontaneity, and the puppet can perform previously unplanned portions of stage-business which occur to the animator while filming.

An additional complication is the necessity of supporting the puppet as he moves. While he might occasionally fly in the air, supported by wires or thread, for the most part the puppet must be securely anchored to the stage to prevent him from falling or vibrating during shooting. The necessity for securing the puppet to the stage affects his gait and restricts his freedom of movement. If the puppet is relatively light in weight it may be possible to apply an adhesive such as rubber cement or spirit gum to the soles of his feet. Loops of masking tape may also be used, the tape being removed when the foot is lifted from the stage and re-applied as the foot comes down again. The feet of puppets are sometimes made of soft materials such as leather, fabric, foam plastic, or rubber. The stage floor is made of fibreboard or some other relatively soft material, and the puppet's feet are secured with pins driven through the top of the foot into the floor. The head of the pin is clipped off below the surface of the foot so that it will not show; when the foot is lifted the pin pulls through and is removed from the table and discarded. With heavier puppets it may be necessary to drive screws up through the floor of the set which screw into the soles of the puppet's feet. However, with this system it is necessary to keep the camera at a low angle so that the holes made in the floor will not be seen by the audience, or to cover the floor of the set with carpet or other material which will close around the holes. Electromagnets have been tried as a means of controlling puppets and holding them on the set. The "kinomatons" used for *Hansel and Gretel,* which are believed to have been designed for Michael Myerberg by engineers at the Fairchild Laboratories, were controlled by electrical solenoids, with electromagnets in the feet. However, the system, which is a closely-guarded trade secret, appears to have been unsatisfactory.

Obviously the production of a puppet film is slow and painstaking. Apart from the pre-production labour of scripting, of building the sets and constructing the puppets, and the post-production work of editing, the actual shooting may require hours of careful work to produce a few seconds of film for the screen. For example: a puppet raises his arm from his side to a horizontal position. He is a miniature, and the arc described by his hand is perhaps three inches. After placing the puppet on the set the animator checks lighting, exposure, camera angle, and other technical elements; then, using his fingers, a push-stick, or tweezers, the animator moves the puppet's arm approximately one quarter of an inch. He then steps back from the set so that he is not in the camera's line of view and is not casting his shadow on the set, and presses the camera control button, making an exposure on the film. He then returns to the set and moves the puppet's arm another quarter of an inch, retires out of range and exposes another frame. A skilful animator might require half an hour to accomplish this repetitive action twenty-four times to produce one second of finished film. It is not surprising that Starevitch only completed his sixty-minute *The Tale of the Fox* ten years after it was begun, and it is interesting to consider that one of the production problems which faced Ptushko in making the feature-length *The New Gulliver* was that Konstantinov, the child-actor who starred in the picture, aged three years during shooting.

Team-work in puppet film production is possible, and is a necessity when many puppets are on camera at the same time. Consideration of the problems involved in finding a number of people who are adept at such work, who can work for protracted periods of time as a smoothly functioning team under the director's guidance, and who do not become bored, distracted, irritable, or careless while working together for a period of days, weeks, or months in the confined space of a puppet studio, gives some insight into the character of persons who undertake this work. The fate of a team-member whose inattention to detail might negate hundreds of man-hours of his teammates' labour is probably better left to the imagination.

CONSTRUCTION AND FORMS

It is a point of some annoyance to animated puppet film enthusiasts to discover that the average filmgoer does not appreciate the differences between an animated puppet film and a film made of a "live" marionette, rod-puppet, or glove-puppet performance. The primary differences are the construction of the puppets and the means by which they are made to move, which ultimately affect the appearance of the film.

Marionettes are loosely-jointed figures which are suspended by thin cords. The operator stands above the puppet and manipulates

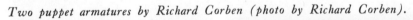
Two puppet armatures by Richard Corben (photo by Richard Corben).

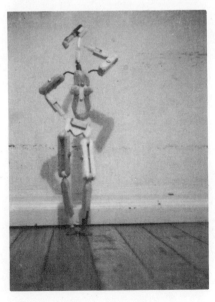

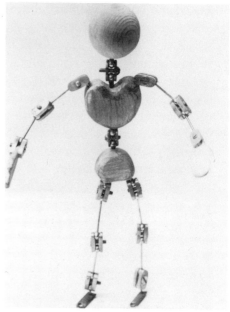

A carved wooden puppet armature by Starevitch (from files of Museum of Modern Art Film Study Center).

A metal armature by David Allen (photo courtesy of Richard Corbin).

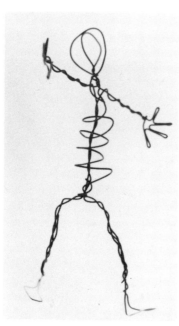

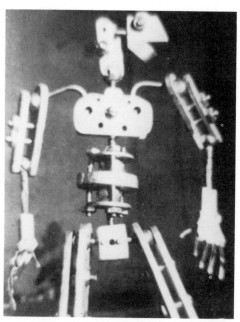

A wood and metal armature (from The National Film Board of Canada, photo by the writer).

A wire armature (by the writer).

the strings to cause the puppet's motions. Rod- and glove-puppets are operated from below the stage, the former being controlled by push-sticks attached to the puppet, while the glove-puppet is fitted over the operator's hand and manipulated by finger and hand movements. These forms of puppets trace their history from ancient times, and since the advent of motion pictures have often been used in producing entertainment and public information films.

The animated puppet is of a different construction since he must be photographed frame-by-frame with an animation camera to produce the appearance of motion. For this work a different type of puppet is necessary. The puppet must be able to stand alone, unsupported by strings or rods while the exposure is being made. The joints of the puppet's limbs need to be flexible enough to permit movement between exposures, yet sufficiently rigid to prevent him from collapsing during a scene. Even minor slippage must be avoided—while the animator might not notice a puppet's arm sagging out of position between exposures, this would appear as an abrupt, unplanned movement in projection. There have been a number of jointing-systems devised to solve this problem.

The most obvious answer for early puppet film-makers was to copy the carved wooden slip-joints used in marionettes, carving them to closer tolerances so that friction enabled the puppet to hold a pose. However, this is not wholly satisfactory since wood-on-wood bearing surfaces soon wear or are polished smooth, and changes in humidity from day to day can cause the joints to expand and become too rigid or contract and slip. Bushings of leather, plastic or metal are of some help, as are adjustable set-screws which can be used to tighten or loosen joints prior to shooting a scene.

It is more satisfactory to use metal joints for animated puppets. Simple slip-joints can be used, but articulated armatures of great complexity have been crafted by puppet animators, involving the use of ball-and-socket and slip-joints held under tension. A carefully-designed armature can duplicate most of the movements of the human body, and can give flawless service for extended periods of time. Reliable metal joints are advisable when the armature is to be embedded in flexible rubber or plastic since a malfunction in the armature of a moulded puppet requires surgery to repair.

One of the simplest articulating systems is the use of flexible wire. An armature of soft iron or pure lead wire of fourteen to eighteen gauge is constructed and padded with cloth or foam materials to the desired proportions. Sometimes pieces of wood or metal are used between joints to provide rigidity where needed. The obvious drawback to the use of wire is that sooner or later the wire will break due to metal fatigue. The useful life of such an armature can be extended by using multiple wires. The animator using this system usually anticipates the problem and provides enough spare puppet bodies to replace those which fall victim to metal fatigue.

Basically there are three types of puppet bodies. The first, which might be called the animated toy, has a body carved or moulded from solid material such as wood or plastic, with flexible or jointed arms, legs, and head added. These are usually painted, with costume details added for decoration. George Pal's puppets were of this type. The second are those puppets which have articulated armatures within a padded body. The joints are usually of metal, with the connecting members being either of metal or wood. If the armature is metal it may form a relatively thin skeleton which is padded with cloth or foam material. The costume covers the padding, and the exposed hands and face are made of wood, rubber, or plastic and are painted to resemble flesh. When wood is used between joints it is often carved to the desired proportions so that little padding is needed under the costume. These are sometimes referred to as "classical" puppets, or as "Czech" puppets since this has been the type generally used in Czechoslovakia. The third type is the moulded puppet, which is made by applying a flexible rubber or plastic body over an articulated armature. The puppet is designed, and an armature is built to the desired size. If the puppet is to be used for an extended period of time, the armature should be sturdy and should use metal joints; if the puppet is to be used only briefly, then a flexible wire armature may suffice. A model of the finished puppet is sculpted with plasticine clay; this may be done either over the actual armature which is to be used for the puppet or over a wire armature of the same proportions. A piece-mould is made of the plasticine model; plaster of Paris is the usual material, although plastics have been used successfully. When the mould is hard it is taken apart, the figure removed, and any remaining pieces of clay cleaned out. If the puppet armature was used for modelling, the clay must be stripped off and the armature cleaned with solvent. The armature is then placed inside the mould, taking care that it is centred and does not touch the mould at any other point except the soles of the feet. Foam rubber or foam plastic is then injected in and allowed to cure. When the foam is cured the puppet is removed from the mould, cleaned, trimmed, and finished for detail. Flexible paints such as latex are used for flesh and features.[25] It is also possible to invest the armature in flexible material by painting it with successive layers of liquid latex until it is built up

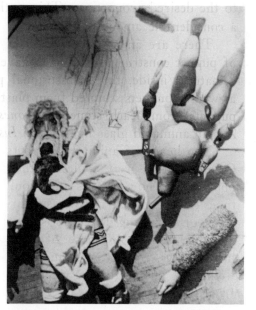

A puppet by B. Pojar (courtesy of The National Film Board of Canada, photo by the writer).

A puppet and armature by Trnka (from files of Museum of Modern Art Film Study Center).

A moulded rubber puppet by David Allen (photo courtesy of Richard Corbin).

A puppet by Trnka for OLD CZECH LEGENDS (photo courtesy of Československý Filmexport).

to the desired proportions. This method requires patience, skill, and a considerable amount of time.

There are an infinite number of variations on these basic types of puppet construction. Puppets have been made like rag dolls with armatures inside, three-dimensional paper puppets have been used, as well as puppets sculpted from plasticine clay. Garik Seko has made puppets from beach stones in *Stones and Life* (1965), and Karel Zeman animated glass figurines in *Inspiration* (1949).

The heads of animated puppets are a matter of some interest. Originally they were copies of the carved wooden heads of theatre puppets, but now plastics and moulded rubber are also used. Sometimes changes of facial expression are necessary, and there are several ways of achieving this. On some puppets the features are made movable, similar to those of very sophisticated marionettes, with hinged jaws, rolling eyes, and the like. However, while this works well in the puppet theatre where the audience is seated some distance from the stage, the close-up view provided by the animation camera often renders this effect stilted or grotesque. The use of movable parts under moulded rubber has been tried and gives a more life-like appearance. Another method is the use of plain faces with painted features which are wiped off and repainted between exposures. This is painstaking work, and care must be taken that the puppet is not knocked from its position. In addition, smudges of paint should not be left since these would photograph as a writhing blotch on the puppet's face. Cut paper features, such as cut eyes and mouth, are also used; these can be applied with rubber cement and removed and replaced as changes of expression are required.

A technique which is often used is the provision of multiple heads for each puppet, each head having a slightly different facial expression. To change a puppet's expression the animator merely lifts off one head and replaces it with another. Depending on the number of heads provided and the rate at which they are changed, facial changes can be gradual or abrupt. A head-change may be obvious to the observer since in addition to the altered expression the puppet's hair and the collar of his costume may be ruffled during the change—this can be an annoying distraction. A similar, though less commonly-used, device is the use of interchangeable face-masks which are keyed to fit a basic puppet head. Ptushko may have used this technique in *The New Gulliver*.[26] Another method is unique to Starevitch: some of the characters in his films have faces made from soft leather; to change expression, particularly around the eyes and mouth, the leather is pushed into new positions between exposures, creating wrinkles and displacement of the features. The effect can be comic or grotesque, but tends toward the latter. The apache character from *The Mascot*, who grimaces and chews on a cigarette butt, is a good example of this technique at work.

A good case can be made for not changing expressions at all. Most of Trnka's puppets use only one head throughout each film, and changes of emotion are achieved by gestures and body-stance. The faces of some of Trnka's characters are designed and painted in such a manner that their expressions and apparent emotional feelings can be completely altered by a shift in lighting and camera-angle. Referring to his use of puppets, Trnka said:

> From the beginning, I had my own conception of how puppets could be handled—each of them to have an individual but static facial expression, as compared with puppets that by means of various technical devices, can change their mien in an attempt to achieve a more life-like aspect. In practice of course, this has tended not to enhance the realism, but rather conduce to naturalism.[27]

However, Ptushko would have disagreed with this:

> The masks of heroes in the doll theatre were immobile, however. They were, so to speak, neutral regarding their inner emotions. Then came to the assistance of the doll theatre the art of multiplication [single-frame puppet animation] with its powerful technique.
> Like a prince in a fairy-tale the cinema put an end to the facial petrifaction of the doll heroes. The art of object multiplication gave dolls the opportunity to acquire all the shades of expression possible to the artist's palette. After a few years of persistent work by a Collective of Soviet artists, our dolls learned to sing of love and joy, to express anger, grief and other emotions called for by the scenario.[28]

Reconciliation of these two views is probably best found by considering the style of each puppet film. If changes of expression are consistent with the tenor of the film, and if the effect is used accordingly, then an additional dimension is available to the animator. Likewise, if a static expression is in keeping with the style which is selected, then the immobile face is easily accepted as a theatrical convention and facial changes are not missed.

In addition to humanoid figures, puppet animators have turned to an incredible variety of materials and objects for use as "puppets." Sticks, stones, match boxes, hardware, and plasticine clay have all been animated. The master of this was Starevitch. Tin cans, egg shells, pieces of straw, and scraps of rags come to life to attend the devil's ball in *The Mascot* (1934), where they dance to an orchestra

From A STUDY IN PAPER (1965) by the author (photo by L. Bruce Holman).

of stuffed toys, rubber balls, and balloons. An actual chicken's skeleton with the bones threaded on flexible wire is a masterpiece of the grotesque, and a set of crystal wine goblets which hop about on spindley legs provide a classic piece of imagery as they fight by smashing themselves against one another. Satan, the host, is knifed by an apache puppet and bleeds sawdust, while the apache throttles a stuffed monkey who has just abducted a drunken toy ballerina. Object animation provides an excellent field for the animator to exercise his imagination.

A simplified version of puppet animation can be done by using a technique similar to flat-figure animation. Instead of flat cut-outs on a horizontal surface under a vertical animation camera, one can make half-round jointed puppets. These are placed flat-side-down on a horizontal sheet of glass and animated by moving them on the glass surface between exposures. The background is placed several inches below the glass, and sufficient light is directed on it to wash out the shadow of the puppet figure above. Although this technique is somewhat easier than animating three-dimensional puppets it has limitations, the most notable being that the puppet must operate in a single plane, and that more than one puppet must be provided if the character is to change from profile to front-face or reverse-profile.

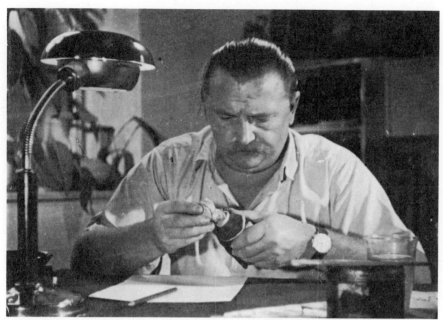

Jiří Trnka constructing a puppet (photo courtesy of Československý Filmexport).

Despite the limitations Břetislav Pojar has used the technique to good effect in some of his recent films, such as *It's Hard to Recognise a Princess*.

SETS, SCENERY AND PROPS

The sets, scenery, and properties used in puppet films have much in common with their counterparts used in live-action films or on the stage. The *décor* must be in keeping with the tenor of the story, and the sets must be useable in terms of the action which is blocked in the script. With the puppet set there are additional considerations which must be kept in mind.

The set must be in scale with the puppet used; that is to say, if the puppet is made to a scale of one-inch-to-one-foot (1″ : 1′) relating to human size, then the scenery and properties must be built to the same scale. A puppet in this scale representing a person of five-and-a-half feet will be five-and-a-half inches tall, and the set to be used will require door openings of about seven by two-and-a-half inches. A two-story building will be approximately sixteen to eighteen inches high. A puppet in 1″ : 1′ scale will be eight-and-a-quarter inches

David Allen sculpting an animated creature (photo by Richard Corbin).

tall and will require door openings of ten-and-a-half by three-and-three-quarter inches.

In constructing the puppet-set scale, practicality, and *décor* are important, but another consideration is its durability. Obviously the set must be strong enough to stand during the time required for shooting, but in addition it must be sturdy enough not to move in the slightest. A gradual, imperceptible swaying of a set wall may not be noticeable during shooting, but could look like a violent earthquake when the film is screened. Sets must be of solid material such as pressed board, plywood, or plaster, and must be well-braced and securely anchored to the base. If the set is to be painted, the paint must be level and non-reflective. Drips, sags, or brush-marks in the paint will be grossly out-of-scale, as will be the shine and highlights caused by a high-gloss paint. The latter will also reflect the set lights, and will appear to flicker from moving reflections of people and equipment in the studio. Flat enamel and lacquer have been used successfully, and latex and acrylic paints should also prove valuable.

The details and degree of finish given to puppet sets and stage-properties must be better than that necessary for live-action sets. Since the camera will be quite close to the set, any flaws will be enormously magnified on the screen. Pojar mentioned that the miniature motorcycle used in *A Drop Too Much* was built with such attention to detail that it cost nearly as much as a real machine.[29]

Consideration must be given to the angle of view of the camera and to the necessity for lighting the set. Particularly in interior sets where the space is restricted to a few square feet, the camera must have a clear field of view and allowances must be made for any planned camera movement. It must also be remembered that the animator requires free access to the puppets on the set. Since he will be reaching into the set to move the puppets space must be provided for this.

Stage properties must also be made to scale, and their design in accord with the style of the film. They should be relatively durable, and if they are to be handled by the puppets they must be light in weight so that they do not drag the puppets out of position while they are being held. Movable properties must be situated so that they will not be knocked out of position by the animator's hands;

Co Hoedeman working on a puppet film set at the National Film Board of Canada (photo by L. Bruce Holman).

it is advisable to secure these with spirit gum, rubber cement, plasticine clay, or pins. "Disturbable" properties and decorations which might ruffle or wrinkle should be avoided, or if their use is necessary they should be handled as little as possible. A fuzzy carpet on a puppet's living room floor may appear to be in a state of twitching agitation because of an occasional accidental brushing of the nap by the animator.

Another troublesome problem is that of dust settling on the set. Since the set may be in use over a prolonged period of time airborn dust particles can gradually accumulate, as well as cobwebs and miscellaneous *débris* accidentally dropped on the set. Not only is dust and dirt on the set bothersome from the standpoint of changing the appearance and the colours, but it also shows marks and fingerprints. A puppet crossing a dusty set may appear to be trailed by a shuffling pattern of scrapes, skuffs, and finger-marks. It is advisable to cover the set with a dropcloth when it is not in use, and to clean it with vacuum hose and soft brush before a day's shooting.

CAMERA

In live-action cinematography changes of camera angle during filming are accomplished with relative ease. Lightweight cameras, smooth-rolling dollies, camera booms, and vari-focal lenses enable the camera to move freely around the subject as the scene is being photographed. In the puppet studio this type of movement is more complicated and requires a high degree of ingenuity to accomplish.

Since the frames of film are being exposed individually the puppet animator does not have the live-action cameraman's freedom to pan, tilt, or move while the camera is running. On the contrary, the animation camera must be absolutely stationary during the time of exposure since movement during the relatively slow shutter time would blur the picture and would cause the image to shake when projected. If camera movement is required—for example, panning to follow a puppet walking across the set—the moving of the camera must be done gradually between exposures. To determine the degree of movement, the distance which the camera is to be shifted is divided by the number of frames of film required to record the movement. The camera movement must be coordinated with the puppet's motion so that the camera neither lags behind nor out-runs the moving puppet, and the motion must be smoothly calibrated to avoid uneven movement.

Live-action cameramen have found that to avoid wrenching starts

From A DROP TOO MUCH (1954) by Bretislav Pojar (photo courtesy of Ceskoslovenský Filmexport).

and sudden, jolting stops, camera movements must be "faired," that is, camera movements must begin slowly, build up to tracking-speed, and gradually decelerate to a halt. Puppet animators must do the same. Additionally, since the puppet and the set are miniatures the camera's motion must be scaled-down correspondingly.[30] An additional complication may arise if the camera motion is too quick: in live-action film the background is usually blurred during fast camera movements although the audience rarely notices this; in animation the background in each frame is sharp and clear. A quick camera movement can produce an annoying staccato-effect known as "strobing."

A variety of mechanical devices have been used to accomplish camera movement, with charts and indicators to plot the camera's required positions during the shot. While the equipment for achieving moving shots is basically similar in all production centres, the specific details vary from studio to studio. Since the demand for this type of mechanism is not sufficiently large to justify commercial manufacture, each is designed and built by studio technicians to suit the studio's particular requirements.

Zoom shots (camera movement into or away from the scene) and tracking shots (lateral camera movement) are achieved by moving the camera on a fixed set of horizontal rails. The rails may be placed on the floor or raised on supports. The camera platform is moved by means of a lead-screw or a rack-and-pinion mechanism, with an indicator to note the degree of movement between exposures. Provision may also be made for vertical camera movement by incorporating a set of vertical rails with a lead-screw for raising and lowering the camera. Vari-focal, or zoom, lenses are now beginning to be used in puppet studios. While the optical effects produced by zooming into or away from a subject are different from the effects produced by dollying the camera, it is unlikely that an audience would be aware of which was used. It is probable that the vari-focal lens, because of its greater convenience, will replace the use of tracks in filming zooms. Tracks will still be necessary for tracking shots, and as a convenient method of positioning the camera.

Panning and tilting the camera is achieved through the use of a geared "head," permitting the apparatus to be pivoted on vertical and horizontal axes. The gear ratio is relatively large so that very fine adjustments can be made in the camera's attitude. The use of a "cradle" mount provides improved rigidity for vertical tilting. In an ideal situation the camera mount should pan and tilt around a pivotal-point located at the focal centre of the camera lens, since this would provide a change in viewing angle without producing an unwanted shift in perspective. This type of mount is not presently available from commercial manufacturers, but since this would be an ideal system for mounting cameras for use in conjunction with the recently-developed reflex-screen background projection system, it is likely that such mounts will be manufactured in the foreseeable future.[31]

It comes as no surprise that camera-movement in puppet films is the exception rather than the rule. Usually the camera is placed securely before the set and remains stationary during the scene; this results in a somewhat static quality in puppet films as compared to contemporary live-action films.

Co Hoedeman has used camera movement effectively in *Odd Ball* (1969), sometimes moving the camera instead of the subject to provide motion which would have been exceedingly difficult to animate. In the end sequence which shows the puppet drifting away atop a rotating ball, the ball is in a fixed location while the camera is backed away on rails. [32] Trnka, as a master of the craft, used camera movement with superb skill when required for cinematic effect. In *The Hand,* the camera moves about the set so smoothly that one is rarely aware that the movement has occurred, apart from noticing changes of angle and perspective. Fifty years earlier Starevitch accomplished

Scene from Trnka's THE HAND (Česk. Filmexport).

camera movement in *The Mascot* by a more direct method—he bodily moved the camera in short jumps from place to place as required for panning and dolly shots. Since the camera was evidently not on rails and the movements calibrated by guess-work, the visual effect was jerky and somewhat startling, but in the context effective—if the viewer's attention was wandering before the movement began, it was certainly arrested and directed to Starevitch's centre of interest by the time the galloping zoom arrived at its object.

In live-action films it is customary to see scenes filmed with the camera situated at approximately the actor's eye-level. For dramatic effect the camera may be raised above or below—the classic example being where one actor (photographed from below) appears to menace another (who is photographed from above). Shooting puppets from their own eye-level gives the audience a feeling of presence—from this point of view they are the same size as the puppets. Shooting from above, the normal viewpoint one would have when looking at miniature puppets, tends to make the audience conscious of the fact that the figures are indeed miniatures. Shooting from below may have approximately the same dramatic effect as in live-action films, but there is a danger the audience may become aware of the effect if it is done obtrusively, and there is something ludicrous about a menacing shot of a puppet who is only a few inches tall.

LIGHTING

The lighting of a puppet set is similar to the lighting of a full-sized set, but some of the principles must be emphasised. Also, errors are easier to make when working with a small set and poorly executed effects will be considerably more obvious when the scene is enlarged in projection.

There is generally a greater need to use lighting to emphasise depth and texture in the puppet set. Although this may be only two feet square, rather than a two acre sound-stage, the film-maker rarely wants to call attention to the fact. By varying the degree of light from one section of the set to another, and by allowing shadows of objects to intersect the set, the impression of space can be increased.

An error which is easy to overlook when working in the restricted space of the puppet set is the casting of multiple shadows from puppets or objects on the set. In nature one is accustomed to seeing objects lit by one primary light source, and one has come to expect the same in films. Multiple shadows are distracting and reveal the use of more than one source of light for the set. Multiple lights are almost always necessary to light the set fully, but the film-maker must remember that each light used will produce a shadow from the object which it is lighting. Unwanted shadows can be countered by using diffused light sources for all but the main light, and by washing out unwanted shadows with additional masked lights.

Because the dramatic abilities of puppets are limited compared to live actors, the use of lighting to augment dramatic effects is an important consideration in emphasising the significance of the actions. It is useful to study the films of Trnka for examples of dramatic lighting in its best applications. In *The Emperor's Nightingale* one may note that darkness is as important as light in setting and maintaining the mood of many of the scenes. The sequence in which Death comes to claim the Emperor is played in half-light or less. Death would be less menacing and the Emperor less pathetic if the set were fully lighted. The morning scene which follows is flooded with bright light, signifying the Emperor's new outlook and his appreciation of life.

There has been a regrettable tendency among some puppet animators to light their sets with a flat, overall, high-key lighting as provided by "scoop" and "broad" lighting units. Considering the effort which is required for other aspects of the production, it is sad to see the effects available through the use of creative lighting ignored to the detriment of the finished film. Over-lighting is understandable when one considers the relative sizes of the small sets and lighting apparatus. A miniature set calls for miniature lighting, but this has not been possible in the past. It must be remembered that there is an optimum quantity of light which must reach the film for correct exposure, no matter how large or small the set. In the past this has required incandescent studio lights. To obtain high light-output from incandescent lights, large bulbs are required, with the attendant problems of large housings and baffles to permit cooling by convection. Thus, to "scale-down" his lighting the puppet animator has had to use the smallest available focusing spotlights, with "snoots," "stovepipes," and "barn doors" to direct the light where it was needed and block it from where it was not wanted.

Another inherent problem with incandescent bulbs is that they become dim with age, causing the colour of the light to change. Microscopic particles evaporate from the wire filament and are precipitated on the inner surface of the glass bulb, blocking a portion of the light. In addition, the filament is reduced in size and the colour of the light is altered, usually toward the red end of the spectrum. In conventional colour cinematography this effect is annoying, since scenes shot one day may not match those shot on another; at least, however, the colour change from scene to scene can generally be

From THE CYBERNETIC GRANDMOTHER (1963) by Jiří Trnka (photo courtesy of Ceskoslovenský Filmexport).

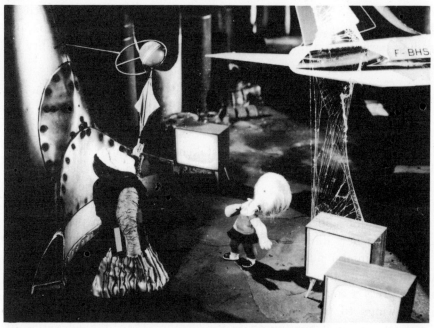

corrected by inserting filters when the film is printed. In puppet animation this effect can be disastrous. A film which runs five minutes may take weeks to produce, allowing ample time for degradation of the lights. The day-to-day change may be too slight to register on photometers and Kelvinometers (used to measure intensity and colour), but it will be all-too-evident when the light changes from a bright blue-white to a dim yellow-orange in five minutes of screen-time. If the effect occurs at a gradual, progressive rate it is exceedingly difficult to correct by filtering. In the past the only way of preventing this was to replace periodically every bulb, with the hope that all new ones would produce the same amount and colour of light. However, with the development of halogen lamps within the past few years, dimming lamps should cease to be a serious problem. The filaments of halogen lamps burn with an intense heat within a gas-filled tube of heat-resistant glass. Instead of vaporising to precipitate inside the glass enclosure, the oxides produced by the heated filament are reduced and return to the filament. Theoretically halogen lamps either burn at the specified intensity and colour or they do not operate at all, so barring the possibility of a lamp failing completely there is little chance for the light to change during shooting. An additional advantage of halogen lamps for puppet animation is their compact size as compared to conventional incandescent lamps. Although they produce ample light for filming, halogen lighting units are small, lightweight, and highly mobile. Their use should eliminate much of the clutter associated with filming in the close quarters of the puppet studio, permitting the animator a greater degree of flexibility in lighting miniature sets.

SOUND

There is a common, although mistaken, impression that prior to the advent of "talking pictures" films were viewed in silence. Musical accompaniment was usually provided in the days before "sound-on-film." However, when the process of printing a soundtrack was perfected, cartoon and puppet films, as well as live-action pictures, had to take this new dimension into account in their production.

It is common practice in cartoon films to record the sound first and then create the drawings to fit the sound. It is difficult to stretch or compress a sound recording, whereas it is easier to create a series of drawings to match a pre-recorded soundtrack. However, since a puppet film is a continuing process rather than a fixed series of drawings, the animator has less latitude—the timing of the puppet's movements becomes much more critical if the movements must synchronise with sound. If the animator is working with a pre-recorded soundtrack, the puppet's movements are to a large degree regulated by the necessity of performing the proper actions at the right time. For example, if a puppet is to fire a gun, and the sound of the shot is recorded thirty seconds from the beginning of the scene, then the animator knows that he has seven hundred and twenty frames in which to raise the puppet's arm. If the calculations are not accurate, the puppet might be in danger of arriving late on cue, in which case the action would have to be rushed, or he might arrive too soon, in which case the animator would have either to slow the action down or invent some impromptu stage-business to cover the wait. If there are multiple or continuous sound-cues and a mistake is made, the scene must be scrapped and begun again. It is generally easier in puppet animation to film the action with reference to a timed pre-recorded soundtrack, and then to re-edit the sound to correspond to the finished film.

If timing of the sound is not critical, it may be preferable to shoot the film first and record the sound later. If the sound is to be post-recorded, the animator has considerably more latitude in handling the puppets during the filming, and greater spontaneity is likely to result.

In addition to the problem of synchronisation, the introduction of dialogue into a puppet film raises the question of whether or not the puppets' mouths are to move as they speak. If they are, either articulated jaws or multiple heads with differing mouth positions must be used. It not, the effect may look stilted or the audience may have difficulty determining which puppet is supposed to be talking.

When dialogue is used there is always the problem of voice characterisation in cartoon and puppet films. Since the figures are usually caricatures of humans, it follows that their voices should not simply be normal human voices, as this would merely draw attention to the fact that the puppets themselves were not the ones speaking the lines. The voices must also be caricatured to be consistant with the characters. Alexis Korobov, the sound engineer for *The New Gulliver,* raised the pitch of the voices one-and-a-half times higher than that of normal speech (presumably by playing-back the recording faster than normal) ; although the dialogue is in Russian, even a non-Russian-speaking audience can appreciate the comic effect of the whining, squeaky voices of the king and his court as counterpoint to their pretentious gestures.

Considering all the problems inherent in using dialogue in puppet films, many animators have concluded that it is simpler and often more effective to eliminate dialogue altogether and rely on pantomime, music, and sound effects to convey meaning. It is probably easier for the audience to derive meaning from the film by watching the action on the screen rather than listening to involved dialogue.

CONTEXT AND CHARACTER

In the traditional Punch and Judy show one of Punch's stock actions consists of belabouring his fellow puppets with a club. This is usually greeted with laughter by the audience, and could be related to a theory of the psychology of slapstick comedy wherein brutality is seen as catharsis or sublimation. However, another explanation is that when Punch is on the puppet stage he is a surrealistic character in a surrealistic world; the unwritten ground-rules say, in effect, that by entering the circle of the puppet theatre the audience has stepped into another world, and it is universally understood that anything which occurs in this world must be accepted by the viewer so long as it conforms to the parameters which have been established. Since all members of the audience are familiar with this convention, it is not necessary to make a conscious effort to suspend disbelief. If Punch beats his dog to death on stage the audience laughs not because they are cruel, but because it is understood that this is merely an expression of Punch's testy temperament and the death of the dog is incidental to the point of the episode; it is equally well-accepted that the dog may come to life in a later scene and bite Punch from behind. Such actions are disturbing only if one forces a conscious return to reality, or an element in the drama is so grossly out of context that the spell is broken. (For example, the introduction of a very realistic stuffed dog instead of the puppet-dog in the beating scene.)

Such conventions apply equally in the animated puppet film. However, there can be any number of styles of these and the film-maker must choose the most suitable: the design of the puppets, and of the sets and decoration, should follow from the nature of the story, and all the elements of the film, including action, stage-business, and pacing, should maintain the established tenor of the work. It would be out of context, for example, if an extremely naturalistic moulded rubber puppet strolled on a set occupied by carved wooden toy puppets. Fast action and quick cutting could be equally disturbing in a film requiring grace and deliberation. For the benefit of the viewer the tone of the work should be established in the first few scenes. Once the viewer is oriented and understands the nature of the film he is watching, he can quickly adapt to its conventions and readily accept the puppets' actions as long as all the elements remain consistent.

When Ptushko decided to use a live actor in conjunction with puppets in *The New Gulliver,* he might have made a decision to make his puppets so life-like that they would not appear ludicrous in comparison. However, considering the nature of the story, it was a far better choice by Ptushko to select an actor who would not appear incongruous. In choosing a child as Petya, the new Gulliver, he reasoned correctly that there would be no inconsistency in a child appearing with puppets in a child's dream-sequence. Later in the film Ptushko made a less fortunate choice in the design of the worker-puppets (designed by Olga Taezhnaya) who revolt against the monarchy. These seem to have all been cast from the same mould (literally as well as figuratively) of a "heroic worker" stereotype, the figures being muscular and rather realistic. Their greater naturalism was intended by Ptushko to serve as counterpoint to the satirical puppets representing the king and his court (designed by Sarah Mokil) and to develop them as identification-figures for Petya and the audience.[33] I do not think this effect works—it is doubtful whether the most ardent revolutionary could identify with these tiny automata. They are totally out of character with either the puppets or the humans in the picture, and represent the only flaw in an otherwise brilliant film.

Establishing context also provides a key to character development. While puppets are not likely to become Stanislavsky method-actors, the motivations for what they do and how they conduct themselves are derived from the situations in which they are depicted. Trnka's cowboy in *Song of the Prairie* (1949) behaves in an exaggeratedly heroic manner because it has been established that he is a caricature of a Hollywood western hero in a parody of that *genre.* Occasionally he may be stupid and require rescue by his horse, but he is always in character. The little potter in Trnka's last film, *The Hand* (1964), is a masterpiece of sympathetic character development. The opening shot of his bedroom-studio with its simple though colourful *décor* suggests that he is a humble but sensitive character, and this is confirmed when he arises and waters the flower on the window ledge, and begins to work at his wheel making more flower pots. Near the end of the film we watch with increasing anxiety as a flower pot teeters on the edge of the dresser above the potter's

Puppets in action: from Jiří Trnka's THE HAND (photo courtesy of Cesko-slovenský Filmexport).

A scene from Trnka's SONG OF THE PRAIRIE (Česk. Filmexport).

head, and wince when it falls and strikes him. He has been developed as a sympathetic character; we understand his problem and admire his fortitude under the threat of the giant hand. Intellectually, we know that he is actually a tiny puppet, yet by consistency of character development Trnka has convinced us that he is real. We feel a sense of loss when he is killed by the falling flower pot, and we are outraged when the Hand hypocritically honours him with a hero's funeral.

AESTHETICS

A generally-accepted tenet of aesthetics is that a work should be in keeping with the medium in which it is executed. However, as Siegfried Kracauer points out in his "Theory of Film," this requires that one define the characteristics of the medium and its parameters. No sooner does one do this than an innovative artist appears and negates all of one's preconceived notions about the limitations of the medium.[34] If one assumes that puppets are by nature wooden and doll-like in their motion, Trnka demonstrates that they can indeed have a high degree of mobility and grace, as evidenced in *A Midsummer Night's Dream* (1959). If it is said that puppets are a medium to themselves, not to be mixed with other forms, then one can point to use of collage with puppets in *The Orator* (1965) and Zeman's effective blend of live actors, photographs, engraving, and puppets in his films.

Be this as it may, there are grounds for making some suggestions regarding the nature of puppet films and what they "should" look like. Consider, for example, the striving for greater realism in puppetry. Great effort and ingenuity has been directed towards designing puppets with jointing systems which permit life-like movement. Cast rubber and plastic materials have been developed in order to give puppet faces and hands the appearance of real flesh, even to the point of embedding springs under rubber skins to simulate muscle movement. Presumably the *reductio ad absurdum* of these experiments would be a puppet whose appearance and movements would be undetectable from those of a human actor—with the obvious rejoinder that it would be simpler and probably less expensive to employ a human actor in the first place. An awkward attempt to push a medium beyond its capacity is generally obvious to the viewer.

Again, this brings the discussion back to the difficulty which Kracauer noted: the question of defining the medium. It is clear that there are "good" puppet films and "poor" puppet films. It is often easy to cite the reasons for the failure of a film—technical errors, poor use of technique, or a lack of imagination on the part of the film-maker—but it is more difficult to define the qualities of a "good" puppet film. A rule-of-thumb might be a consideration of the factor of "poetic economy." Poetic economy relates to the solution in a problem-solving situation, and is useful as a conceptual tool in judging the merits of a solution. If the creation of a work of art is viewed as essentially a problem-solving situation, the characteristics of poetic economy provide criteria for criticism. In this context it is not sufficient to devise a solution which is merely expedient; the poetically economical solution is that which best deals with the attendant conditions of the problem, effectively utilises the resources at hand, and leaves no "loose ends" unaccounted. Attendant to, or inherent, in this solution is a feeling of aesthetic satisfaction.

In relation to puppet animation, Trnka's remarks would seem to be in keeping with this viewpoint:

> I had . . . an ambition to animate on the screen, where everything is possible, the three-dimensional figures of puppets, moving in contradistinction to the heroes of cartoons, not within their own plane but in space. From the beginning, I had my own conception of how puppets could be handled— each of them to have an individual but static facial expression, as compared with the puppets that by means of various technical devices, can change their mien in an attempt to achieve a more life-like aspect. In practice of course, this has tended not to enhance the realism, but rather conduce to naturalism. . . .
>
> Puppet films stand on their own feet only when they are outside the scope of live-action films—when the stylisation of the scenery, the artificially heroic look of the human actors, and the lyrical content of the theme might easily produce an effect both unconvincing and ludicrous or even painful.[35]

In other words, a puppet is a puppet. He is neither a live actor nor a cartoon film character, he is unique and in a medium of his own. To force puppet animation beyond its point of efficiency by over-elaboration, or to waste carelessly the potentials which puppets possess, are violations of the principle of poetic economy. This is not to say that the last puppet film has been made nor must all others follow the forms which have already been established; there is ample latitude for experimentation and innovation within the field. The integrity of the medium, however, should be respected. Style and presentation, and much of the form itself, may change, but there should not be a conscious attempt to imitate other media, nor should puppet animation be forced into a configuration to which it does not lend itself.

From THE LION AND THE SONG *(circa 1958), by Bretislav Pojar (photo courtesy of Ceskoslovenský Filmexport).*

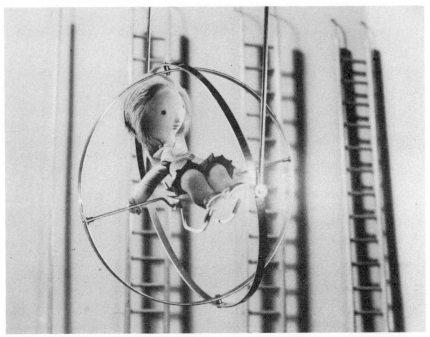

Scene from Trnka's THE CYBERNETIC GRANDMOTHER *(Česk. Filmexport).*

FILMOGRAPHIES

REPRESENTATIVE FILMOGRAPHY
OF WORLD PUPPET FILM PRODUCTION

About a Comb Who Didn't Want To Brush His Teeth, Poland, 1967.
About Bachtalo, the Gypsy, Krystyna Dobrowolska, Poland, 1967.
About Johnny Who Made Shoes For Dogs, Lidia Hornicka, Poland, 1962.
Accident, An (puppet with live actors), Hermína Týrlová, Czech., 1948.
Adventure In Space, Hans Ulrich Wiemer, East Germany.
Adventures In a Cupboard, Edward Sturlis, Poland, 1965.
Adventures Of An Alarm-Clock, Jania Hartwig, Poland, 1962.
Adventures Of Mr. Pry, The (cartoon and puppet), Karel Dodal and Hermína Týrlová, Czech., 1936.
Aladdin and the Wonderful Lamp, George Pal, Great Britain, *ca.* 1936.
Alarm, Teresa Badzian, Poland, 1965.
"Alexeieff Advertising Films" (puppet and cartoon for Paris Exposition), Alexander Alexeieff, France, 1937.
Ali Baba, George Pal, Great Britain, 1936.
Alice In Wonderland, Louis Bunin, Great Britain, 1951.
All Quiet In the East, P. Bianchi, France, 1934.
Alsort Ballet, J. Barton, Great Britain, *ca.* 1956.
And To Think I Saw It On Mulberry Street, George Pal, U.S.A., 1944.
Angel and Man, Edward Sturlis, Poland, 1967.
Anton the Musician, Günter Rätz, East Germany, 1967.
Ape, The, Yang Tei, China(?), 1959.
Apostle, The, Günter Rätz, East Germany, 1965.
Archangel Gabriel and Mother Goose, Jiří Trnka, Czech., 1965.
Askeladd, Ivo Caprino, Norway.
At the End Of the Road, Wang Chou-Tchez, China, 1966.
Automatic Moving Company, The (Mobelier fidèle), Emile Cohl, France, 1910.
Aviation, Günter Rätz, East Germany, 1966.
Bad Little Fox, The, Zenon Wasilewski, Poland, 1951.
Bad Magician, The, Alvar Eriksson, Sweden.
Barrel-Organ, The, Haupe and Bielińska, Poland, 1965.
Barrel-Organ, The, J. Kotowski, Poland, *ca.* 1960.
Basilisk, The, L. Serafinowicz and W. Wieczorkieloica, Poland, 1962.
Bath House, The, Sergey Yutkevich and Anton Karanovich, U.S.S.R., 1962.
Bed Bug, The, A. Ptushko, U.S.S.R., *ca.* 1931.
Berceuse, Hermína Týrlová, Czech., 1948.
Bill Has a Hundred Faces, István Imre, Hungary, 1969.
Billiards, Břetislav Pojar, Czech., 1964.
Bimbo, Erich Hammer, East Germany.
Birth Of a Robot, Len Lye and Humphrey Jennings, Great Britain, 1936.
Birth Of the Host Of the Forest, The, Ladislas Starevitch, Russia, *ca.* 1912.
Black King, The, Jerzy Kotowski, Poland, 1962.

Black Love and White Love, Ladislas Starevitch, France, *ca.* 1927.
Blue Beard, Jean Painlevé and René Bertrand, France, 1938.
Blue Duckling, The, Lucjan Dembiński, Poland, 1967.
Blue Pinafore, The, Hermína Týrlová, Czech., 1966.
Boastful Knight, The, Edward Sturlis, Poland, 1955
Boy Or the Girl, The, Hermína Týrlová, Czech., 1966.
"Bratishkin" series, A. Ptushko, U.S.S.R., *ca.* 1931.
Bravo Mr. Strauss, George Pal, U.S.A., 1943.
Breaking Of Branches Is Forbidden, Kihachiro Kawamoto, Japan, 1969.
Budulinek and the Foxes, V. Zykmund and A. Vesela, Czech.
Button, The, Teresa Badzian, Poland, 1965.
Cactus, L. Dembiński, Poland, *ca.* 1960.
Captain, Kurt Weiler, East Germany.
Card Maniac, The, Richard Teschner, Austria, 1930.
Carnival Dress, Kurt Weiler, East Germany.
Carrot Nose, Kurt Weiler, East Germany.
Cat and the Sphinx, The, Louis Bunin, U.S.A., 1969.
Cats and Kittens, Tadeusz Wilosz, Poland, 1965.
Cat's World Of Honour, A (cut paper), Břetislav Pojar, Czech., 1963.
Celestial Creature, The, Natason Obrastsa, U.S.S.R.
Changing Of the Guard, Bielińska and Haupe, Poland, 1959.
Christmas Dream, Karel Zeman, Czech., 1946.
Christmas Sonnet, Hermína Týrlová, Czech., 1968.
Christmas Tree, Hermína Týrlová, Czech., 1968.
Circus Hurvinek, Jiří Trnka, Czech., 1955.
City Rat and the Country Rat, The, Ladislas Starevitch, France, 1927.
Claws Of the Spider, The, Ladislas Starevitch, France, 1924.
Clay, Elliot Noyse, U.S.A., 1964.
Cloud Sheep, The, Katja Georgi, East Germany.
Clumsey Little Elephant, The, Günter Rätz, East Germany.
Cock, The, Lucjan Dembiński, Poland, 1966.
Cock Crows At Midnight, The, Yeou Lei, China, 1966.
Come and Play, Sir (series of three), Břetislav Pojar, Czech., 1965–67.
Commune, A, Ewa and Olga Totwen, Poland, 1954.
Commune Effort, A, Olga Totwen, Poland, 1953.
Concurrence, Katja Georgi, East Germany, 1965.
Congratulations, Günter Rätz, East Germany, 1965.
Coster Bill Of Paris (puppet sequence by Starevitch), Jacque De Baroncelli, France, 1933.
Course For Husbands, Vladimir Lehky, Czech., 1961.
Course For Wives, Vladimir Lehky, Czech., 1962.
Courting Songs, Louis Bunin, U.S.A., 1955.
Cracked Ice, Edwin Miles Fadman, U.S.A., 1924.
Crane's Magic Gift, The, Gakken Company, Japan.
Crime On Cat-the-Ventriloquist Street, The, Zenon Wasilewski, Poland, 1962.
Crooked Chimney, The, Pavel Prochazka, Czech., 1970.
Cubes Ole, Richard Thomas, U.S.A., 1970.
Cupid's Arrow, Ladislas Starevitch, France, *ca.* 1935,
Curiosity, Günter Rätz, East Germany, 1966.

From *THE BLUE PINAFORE (1966)*, by Hermína Týrlová (photo courtesy of Ceskoslovenský Filmexport).

Cybernetic Grandmother, The, Jiří Trnka, Czech., 1963.
Czech Year, The, Jiří Trnka, Czech., 1947.
Damon, Edward Sturlis, Poland.
Date With Duke, George Pal, U.S.A., *ca.* 1940–1949.
Deceived Fox, The, Bob Calinescu, Romania, 1952.
Demon, The, Lucjan Dembiński, Poland, 1967.
Devil's Dirty Work, The, George D'Bomba, East Germany, 1962.
Devil's Mill, The, Jiří Trnka, Czech., 1951.
Devil's Valley, The, Katja Georgi, East Germany, 1959.
Dingo Dog and the Kangaroo, The, Louis Bunin, U.S.A., 1962.
Dinosaur and the Missing Link, The, Willis H. O'Brien, U.S.A., *ca.* 1917.
Dipsy Gypsy, George Pal, U.S.A., 1940.
Dogs Heaven, Hermína Týrlová, Czech., 1967.
Dolly Doings, Howard S. Moss, U.S.A., *ca.* 1917.
Donkey Prince, The, Zenon Wasilewski, Poland.
Dragon Of Kraków, The, Zenon Wasilewski, Poland, 1946.
Drake, Stefan Topalogikov, Bulgaria.
Drawing For Cats (cut paper), Břetislav Pojar, Czech., 1963.
Dreams Of Toyland, Arthur Melbourne Cooper, Great Britain, 1908.
Drop Too Much, A, Břetislav Pojar, Czech., 1954.
Duet, Vladimir Lehky, Czech., 1968.
Dunkling Of the Circus, Howard S. Moss, U.S.A., *ca.* 1917.
East, West, Home Is Best, Josef Kluge, Czech., 1970.
Egg, The, Heinz Steinbach, East Germany.
Emperor's New Clothes, The, Kurt Herbert Schulz, East Germany, 1958.
Emperor's Nightingale, The, Jiří Trnka, Czech., 1948.
Enchanted Wampum, The, Lidia Hornicka, Poland, 1965.

From Trnka's THE HAND (photo courtesy of Československý Filmexport).

Escape, Lucjan Debiński, Poland, 1965.
Ether Ship, George Pal, Holland, 1935.
Eva and the Grasshopper, Diehl Brothers, Germany, 1928.
Everyone Helps Teddy, Monika Anderson, East Germany.
Evil Magician, The, Alvar Eriksson, Sweden.
"Experimental Animation", Len Lye, Great Britain, 1933.
Eyes Of the Dragon, The, Ladislas Starevitch, France, 1927.
Fairy Ring, The, Tadeusz Wilkosz, Poland, 1966.
False Alarm, Johannes Hempel, East Germany.
Ferda the Ant, Hermína Týrlová, Czech., 1942.
Ferko the Pouch, Hermína Týrlová, Czech., 1968.
Fern Flowers, Ladislas Starevitch (with Sonika Bo), France, 1950.
Figaro, Heinz Steinbach, East Germany.

Figurehead, Halas and Batchelor, Great Britain, 1953.
Fips the Trouble-Maker, Johannes Hempel, East Germany.
Five Hundred Hats Of Bartholomew Cubbins, George Pal, U.S.A., 1943.
Flying Frogs, The, Velichko, U.S.S.R.
Flying Insects, Ladislas Starevitch, Russia, *ca.* 1912.
Folksong Fantasy, Alma Duncan, Canada, *ca.* 1957.
For Pete's Sake, Lidia Hornicka, Poland, 1966.
Forgotten Doll, The, Johannes Hempel, East Germany.
Fox and Hedgehog, Hans Ulrich Wiemer, East Germany.
Frogs Who Wanted a King, The, Ladislas Starevitch, France, 1923.
Game, A, Teresa Badzian, Poland, 1967.
Garland of Folk-Songs, A, Hermína Týrlová, Czech., 1955.
Gardinentraum, Der (Curtain-Dream), Katja Georgi and Heinrich-Greif-
    Preistragger, East Germany, 1969.
Ghost Can't Take It, The, Lidia Hornicka, Poland, *ca.* 1960.
Ghost In the Village, The, Erich Hammer, East Germany.
Gingerbread Cottage, The, (puppets by Trnka), Břetislav Pojar, Czech., 1951.
Gingerbread Kingdom, The, Zenon Wasilewski, Poland.
Go East, Young Woman, J. Barton, Great Britain, pre-1957.
Goat and the Hedgehog, The, V. Zykmund and A. Vesela, Czech.
Golden Key, The, A. Ptushko, U.S.S.R., 1939.
Goldilocks (Golden Curls), Hermína Týrlová, Czech., 1955.
Goldilocks and the Three Bears, Howard S. Moss, U.S.A., 1917.
Good Day Mr. H., Katja Georgi, East Germany, 1965.
Goodnight Rusty, George Pal, U.S.A., 1943.
Good Soldier Schweik, Jiří Trnka, Czech., 1954.
Gooseberry Pie, George Pal, U.S.A., *ca.* 1940–1949.
Grasshopper and the Ant, The, Ladislas Starevitch, Russia, 1911.
Gumbasia, Art Clokey, U.S.A., 1955.
Hamster, The, Karel Zeman, Czech., 1946.
Hand, The, Jiří Trnka, Czech., 1965.
Hansel and Gretel, Michael Myerberg Productions, U.S.A., 1954.
Happy Circus, The, Jiří Trnka, Czech., 1951.
Happy Man, The, Stefan Topalogikov, Bulgaria, 1961.
Happy Scenes In the Life Of the Animals, Ladislas Starevitch, Russia, *ca.* 1912.
Harlequin Nimbo, The, Zenon Wasilewski, Poland, *ca.* 1947–1950.
Hats Down!, Stefan Topalogikov, Bulgaria, 1960.
Haunted Hotel, The, (object animation), James Stuart Blackton, U.S.A., 1907.
Haunted Studio, The, Johannes Hempel, East Germany.
Hold-Up, The, Johannes Hempel, East Germany.
Hold Your Hats, Břetislav Pojar, Czech., 1967.
Homer, the Horse Who Couldn't Talk, Louis Bunin, U.S.A., 1958.
Honey Comb, A, Jerzy Kotowski, Poland, 1965.
Horseshoe For Luck, A, Karel Zeman, Czech., 1947.
How To Furnish a Flat, Břetislav Pojar, Czech., *ca.* 1958–1962.
Human Foolishness, G. Sibianu, Romania, *ca.* 1968.
Ideal, Břetislav Pojar, Czech., 1965.
Inquisitive Letter, The, Hermína Týrlová, Czech., 1961.
Inspiration, Karel Zeman, Czech., 1949.

In the Jungle, Howard S. Moss, U.S.A., *ca.* 1917.
In the Land Of the Vampires, Ladislas Starevitch, France, 1935.
Introductory Speech Is By . . . , The, Břetislav Pojar, Czech., 1964.
It's a Fiasco, Gentlemen, B. Pojar and Miroslav Stephanek, Czech, 1970.
It's Hard To Recognise a Princess, Břetislav Pojar, Czech., 1968.
Janosik, Haupe and Bielińska, Poland, 1953.
Jasper and the Beanstalk, George Pal, U.S.A., 1945.
Jasper and the Choo Choo, George Pal, U.S.A., 1943.
Jasper and the Haunted House, George Pal, U.S.A., 1942.
Jasper and the Watermelons, George Pal, U.S.A., 1942.
Jasper Goes Fishing, George Pal, U.S.A., 1943.
Jasper Goes Hunting, George Pal, U.S.A., 1944.
Jasper's Booby Trap, George Pal, U.S.A., 1945.
Jasper's Close Shave, George Pal, U.S.A., 1945.
Jasper's Derby, George Pal, U.S.A., 1946.
Jasper's Minstrels, George Pal, U.S.A., 1945.
Jasper's Music Lesson, George Pal, U.S.A., 1943.
Jasper's Paradise, George Pal, U.S.A., 1944.
Jasper Tell, George Pal, U.S.A., 1945.
Jimmy Gets the Pennant, Howard S. Moss, U.S.A., *ca.* 1917.
John Henry and the Inky-Poo, George Pal, U.S.A., 1946.
Jorinde and Joringel, Johannes Hempel, East Germany.
Joseph and His Brethren, Israel, 1962.
Journey Into Prehistory (live action with special effects), Karel Zeman, Czech.,
    1955.
Katherine and the Hangman, Katarzyna Latałło, Poland, 1966.
Kids On a Belfry, Jania Hartwig, Poland, 1965.
King Lavra, Karel Zeman, Czech., 1950.
King Midas, Edward Sturlis, Poland.
King Of the Animals, The, Günter Rätz, East Germany, 1960.
King's Sentence, The, Katarzyna Latałło, Poland, 1962.
Kitchen Romance, A, Howard S. Moss, U.S.A., *ca.* 1917.
Knot In the Handkerchief, The, Hermína Týrlová, Czech., 1958.
Kumak the Sleepy Hunter, Alma Duncan, Canada, 1958.
Kutasek and Kutilka, Jiří Trnka, Czech., 1952.
Lajkonik, M. Kruger, Poland, *ca.* 1960.
Lake Of the Fairies, Gheorghe Sibianu, Romania, 1963.
Lantern Mystery, The, Karel Dodal and Hermína Týrlová, Czech., 1938.
Lazy Martin, Hermína Týrlová, Czech., 1957.
Lesson, A, Hermína Týrlová, Czech., 1960.
Lion and the Gnat, The, Ladislas Starevitch, France, *ca.* 1930.
Lion and the Song, The, Břetislav Pojar, Czech., *ca.* 1958.
Little Bead Fish, The, Hermína Týrlová, Czech., 1968.
Little Bear's Journey, Rasa Strautman, U.S.S.R., *ca.* 1966.
Little Black Sambo, George Pal, U.S.A., *ca.* 1944.
Little Boy Doesn't Wash, The, Edward Sturlis, Poland, 1955.
Little Frikk, Ivo Caprino, Norway.
Little Giraffe, The, Teresa Badzian, Poland, *ca.* 1960.
Little Girl and the Naughty Fairy, The, Japan.

From Bretislav Pojar's teddy bear series (photo courtesy of Československý Filmexport).

Little Haewelmann, Kurt Herbert Schulz, East Germany.
Little Hare and the Well, The, Johannes Hempel and Ina Rarisch, East Germany.
Little Kangaroo, The, Teresa Badzian, Poland, 1967.
Little Kate, Hermína Týrlová, Czech., 1962.
Little Music, Teresa Badzian, Poland, 1962.
Little Pig, The, Zenon Wasilewski, Poland, 1960.
Little Quartet, A, Edward Sturlis, Poland, 1966.
Little Soldier, Paul Grimault, France, 1947.
Little Street-Singer, The, Ladislas Starevitch, 1923.
Little Train, The, Hermína Týrlová, Czech., 1959.
Little Umbrella, The, Břetislav Pojar, Czech., 1958.
Little Woodcutter, The, People's Republic of China.
Lost Doll, The, Hermína Týrlová, Czech., 1959.
Lost Sentry, The, Miloš Makovec, Czech.
Love On the Range, George Pal, Great Britain, 1938.
Lovers In the South Seas, George Pal, Great Britain, 1938.
Lullaby, Hermína Týrlová, Czech., 1947.
Magic Atlas, The, George Pal, Holland, ca. 1935.
Magic Bow, The, Kurt Herbert Schulz, East Germany.
Magic Box, The, Stefan Topalogikov, Bulgaria, 1958.
Magic Brush, The, Wan Tchao-Tchen, China (?).
Magic Cask, The, Kurt Herbert Schulz, East Germany.
Magic Clock, The, Ladislas Starevitch, France, 1928.
Magic Gift, The, Zenon Wasilewski, Poland, 1956.
Magic Hoe, The, Stefan Topalogikov, Bulgaria, 1960.
Magic Pencil, The, Tsin Si, China (?), 1954.
Magic Pig, The, Howard S. Moss, U.S.A., 1917.

Man From the Mirror, A, Zenon Wasilewski, Poland, 1967.
Manguar, Edward Sturlis, Poland, *ca.* 1960.
Man Who Wanted To Fly, The, Gakken Company, Japan.
Marble, The, Hermína Týrlová, Czech., 1963.
Marriage Of Babylas, The, Ladislas Starevitch, France, *ca.* 1920.
Mascot, The, Ladislas Starevitch, France, 1934.
Matches, Katja Georgi, East Germany, 1962.
Matrioska, Co Hoedeman, Canada, 1969.
Measure For Measure, Günter Rätz, East Germany.
Meeting, The, Jana Olexová, Czech., 1970.
Merry-Go-Round, The, A. Vesela and V. Zykmund, Czech.
Micro the Invisible, Stefan Topalogikov, Bulgaria.
Midnight, George Pal, Germany, *ca.* 1932.
Midnight Frolic, Howard S. Moss, U.S.A., *ca.* 1917.
Midnight Incident, Břetislav Pojar, Czech., *ca.* 1958–1962.
Midsummer Night's Dream, A, Jiří Trnka, Czech., 1959.
Miraculous Spring, The, Edward Sturlis, Poland, 1967.
Misfit Figure, The, Hermína Týrlová, Czech., 1950.
Misha the Ball, Hermína Týrlová, Czech., 1956.
Mistress Holle, Johannes Hempel, East Germany.
Mitten, The, U.S.S.R., 1968 (?).
Mose and Funny Face Make Angel Cake, Edwin Miles Fadman, U.S.A., *ca.* 1924.
Mr. Elephant, Teresa Badzian, Poland, *ca.* 1960.
Mr. Lens and the Wilderness, J. Kotowski, Poland, *ca.* 1960.
Mr. Plume Has a Dream, Zenon Wasilewski, Poland, *ca.* 1947–1950.
Mr. Prokouk and the Red Tape (Mr. Prokouk Bureaucrat), Karel Zeman, Czech., 1949.
Mr. Prokouk Animal Fancier, Karel Zeman, Czech., 1955.
Mr. Prokouk, Detective, Karel Zeman, Czech., 1957.
Mr. Prokouk In the Circus, Karel Zeman, Czech., 1959.
Mr. Prokouk, Inventor, Karel Zeman, Czech., 1948.
Mr. Prokouk On a Brigade, Karel Zeman, Czech., 1948.
Mr. Prokouk's Temptation, Karel Zeman, Czech., 1947.
Mr. Servadac's Ark, Karel Zeman, Czech., 1968.
Musical Box, The, Jerzy Kotowski, Poland, 1969.
Musicians, Katja Georgi, East Germany, 1963.
Musicians In the Woods, Japan.
Naughty Chicken, The, Stefan Topalogikov, Bulgaria, 1962.
Navigator, The, Ladislas Starevitch, France, 1934.
Negrita's Island, Gheorghe Sibianu, Romania, 1957.
Never Tease a Lion, T. Wilkosz, Poland, *ca.* 1960.
New Gulliver, The, A. Ptushko, U.S.S.R., 1935.
New House, The, Teresa Badzian, Poland, 1955.
Night In the Picture Gallery, A. Tovarek and J. Zdrubecký, Czech.
Night Of Surprises, A, Jania Hartwig, Poland, 1966.
Nine Chickens, The, Hermína Týrlová, Czech., 1952.
Noah's Ark, Arthur Melbourne Cooper, Great Britain, 1908.
Noah's Ark, Disney Studio, U.S.A., 1959.

Nobi, Günter Rätz, East Germany.
Nocturnal Romance, A, Hermína Týrlová, Czech., 1949.
Noise, Zofia Wdowkówna-Oldak, Poland, 1965.
Oddball, Co Hoedeman, Canada, 1969.
Old Czech Legends, Jiří Trnka, Czech., 1953.
Old Lion, The, Ladislas Starevitch, France, 1932.
Olde Bangum, Louis Bunin, U.S.A., 1955.
One Little Indian, Alma Duncan, Canada, *ca.* 1960.
On Light, B. Sramek, K. Lhotak, and V. Sivko, Czech.
On Parade, George Pal, Great Britain, 1936.
Operation Proxima Centauri, Jörg D'Bombá, East Germany.
Orator, The, Břetislav Pojar, Czech., 1965.
Orchard Of Père Laurent, The, Haupe and Bielińska, Poland, 1952.
Orpheus and Eurydice, Edward Sturlis, Poland, 1962.
Out In the Rain, Howard S. Moss, U.S.A., *ca.* 1917.
Package For Jasper, George Pal, U.S.A., 1944.
Painting, Hermína Týrlová, Czech., 1970.
Paper Cock-a-Doodle (trick film with cut-out paper birds), Pathé Brothers, France, 1908.
Passion, The (Obsession), Jiří Trnka, Czech., 1962.
Pawel and Gawel, R. Potocki, Poland, 1946.
Peacock Princess, The, People's Republic of China, *ca.* 1967.
Peasant Careless, Johannes Hempel, East Germany.
Pete Roleum and His Cousins, Joseph Losey and Howard Bay, U.S.A., 1939.

From PAINTING (1970), by Hermína Týrlová (photo courtesy of Ceskoslovenský Filmexport).

Petit Chantecler, Le, Edmond Rostand, France.
Petit Faust, Le, Emile Cohl, France, 1910.
Petite Parade, The, Ladislas Starevitch, France, 1929.
Philips Cavalcade, Joop Geesink, Holland, 1964.
Philips On Parade, Joop Geesink, Holland, 1967.
Photography, Günter Rätz, East Germany, 1965.
Pimpinella, Germany.
Place, The, Edward Sturlis, Poland, 1966.
Plastic In the Park, Katja Georgi, East Germany, 1964.
Play and Work, A. Ptushko, U.S.S.R., *ca.* 1931.
Plumbers, Zofia Wdowkówna-Oldak, Poland, 1962.
Poo Poo Puppet Series, The, George Gros.
Precursor, The, Zofia Wdowkówna-Oldak, Poland, 1966.
Prehistoric Poultry: The Dinornis Or the Great Roaring Whiffenpoof, Willis
      O'Brien, U.S.A., 1917.
Prince Bajaja, Jiří Trnka, Czech., 1950.
Prince Electron, Joop Geesink Studio, Holland.
Princess and the Dragon, The, Zenon Wasilewski, Poland.
Princess and the Pea, The, Katja Georgi, East Germany, 1959.
Prsh and Drsk, Czech.
Problem, The, Jan Dudeske, Czech.
Puppet Parade, The, Hermína Týrlová, Czech., 1956.
Puppet's Dream, The, Al Sens, Canada, *ca.* 1958.
Puss In Boots, Diehl Brothers, Germany, 1938.
Pyramid, The, Katja Georgi, East Germany, 1961.
Queen Of the Butterflies, The, Ladislas Starevitch, France, *ca.* 1928.
Race, The, Günter Rätz, East Germany.
Race Of the Rabbit and the Hedgehog, The, Diehl Brothers, Germany, pre-1938.
Rascal Snail, The, Haupe and Bielińska, Poland, 1951.
Raven, The, Canada.
Revenge Of the Kinematographic Cameraman, Ladislas Starevitch, Russia, *ca.*
      1912.
Revolt Of the Toys, Hermína Týrlová, Czech., 1947.
R.F.D. 1000 B.C., Willis H. O'Brien, U.S.A., 1917.
Rhapsody In Wood, Bob Calinescu, Romania, 1960.
Rhythm In the Ranks, George Pal, U.S.A., 1941.
Ringmaster, The, Ladislas Starevitch, France, *ca.* 1933.
Robber Baron In the Country, Jörg D'Bombá, East Germany.
Rolling Rice Ball, The, Gakken Company, Japan.
Romance, Břetislav Pojar, Czech., 1965.
Romeo and Juliet, Hermína Týrlová, Czech., 1958.
Sack, The, Tadeusz Wilkosz, Poland, 1967.
Scarecrow, The, Ladislas Starevitch, France, 1921.
School Days, Howard S. Moss, U.S.A., *ca.* 1917.
School For Cats (cut paper), Břetislav Pojar, Czech., 1963.
Scissors, František Vystrčil, Czech., 1970.
Scrap Of Paper and a Piece Of String, A, John Korty, U.S.A., 1964.
Sculptress Of Policka, The, Jaroslav Boček, Czech., 1970.
Secret Path, The, Kurt Weiler, East Germany.

Secret Way, The, Herbert K. Schulz, East Germany, 1958.
Selfish Giant, The, David Allen, U.S.A., *ca.* 1969.
Seven Ravens, The, Diehl Brothers, Germany, 1937.
Shadow Of Time, Jerzy Kotowski, Poland, 1965.
Shah's Magic Beard, The, Bogdan Nowicki, Poland, 1967.
Sharp Left Behind the Moon, Günter Rätz, East Germany.
Ship Of Ether, George Pal, Holland, *ca.* 1935.
Sinbad, George Pal, Great Britain, 1935.
Sky Pirates, George Pal, Great Britain, 1938.
Sleeping Beauty, The, Alexander Alexeieff, France, 1935.
Small Banknote, Wacław Krukowski, Poland, 1966.
Snowman, Hermína Týrlová, Czech., 1966.
Song of the Dove, Günter Rätz, East Germany, 1960.
Song of the Prairie, Jiří Trnka, Czech., 1949.
Spaarroussel, Joop Geesink, Holland, 1967.
Speijbl On the Track, Břetislav Pojar, Czech., 1958.
Stag-Beetles, The, Ladislas Starevitch, Russia, *ca.* 1911.
Stairs, Stefan Schabenbeck, Poland, 1969.
Star of Bethlehem, The, Hermína Týrlová, Czech., 1969.
Status, Edward Sturlis, Poland.
Steadfast Tin Soldier, The, Ivo Caprine, Denmark.
Stolen Nose, The, Kurt Weiler, East Germany.
Stone and Life, Garik Seko, Czech., *ca.* 1965.
Stork and the Fox, The, Zenon Wasilewski, Poland, 1951.
Story About Santa Claus, A, Monika Anderson, East Germany.
Story Of a Little Girl Who Wanted To Be, Ladislas Starevitch, France, *ca.* 1919.
Story of Michalkowice, The, Zenon Wasilewski, Poland, 1955.
Story of the Double-Bass, The, Jiří Trnka, Czech., 1949.
Story Of the Five Brothers, The, Kurt Weiler, East Germany.
Story of the Matches, The, Johannes Hempel, East Germany.
Strange History of the Citizens of Schilt, The, Johannes Hemple, East Germany.
Strange Voyage, The, Teresa Badzian, Poland, 1955.
Street Is Not a Playground, The, Hans Ulrich Weimer, East Germany.
Study In Paper, L. Bruce Holman, U.S.A., 1965.
Surprise, The, Teresa Badzian, Poland, 1966.
Swan Lake, Stefan Topalogikov, Bulgaria, 1965.
Sweet-Toothed Budulinek, V. Zykmund and A. Vesela,. Czech.
Swineherd, The, Hermína Týrlová, Czech., 1958.
Tale Of the Fox, The, Ladislas Starevitch, France, 1929–1939.
Tales and Yarns, Johannes Hempel, East Germany.
Taming Of the Dragon, The, Hermína Týrlová, Czech., 1953.
Tangle, The, Katarzyna Latałło and Wiesław Antosik, Poland, 1967.
Tea-Pot, The, Haupe and Bielińska, Poland, 1962.
Teddy Brumm, Günter Rätz, East Germany, 1958.
Thieves, The, W. Kondek, Poland, *ca.* 1960.
Thorn, The, Katja Georgi, East Germany, 1967.
Three Heroes, The, Stefan Topalogikov, Bulgaria, 1964.
Three Wishes, Günter Rätz, East Germany, 1967.

Till Eulenspiegel As Watchman, Johannes Hempel, East Germany.
Till Eulenspiegel and the Baker Of Brunswick, Johannes Hempel, East Germany.
Times Of King Krakus, The, Zenon Wasilewski, Poland, *ca.* 1947.
Tiny Tot, The, Lucjan Dembiński, Poland, 1966.
Top Dog (from *Snip and Snap* series), Halas and Batchelor, Great Britain.
To See Or Not To See, Břetislav Pojar, Czech., 1968.
Toyland Topics, Great Britain, *ca.* 1928.
Tragedy In Toyland, A, Kalem Company, U.S.A., 1911.
Travelling Tune, The, Joop Geesink, Holland, 1960.
Treasure Of Bird Island, The, Karel Zeman, Czech., 1952.
Trip To the Moon, A, Howard S. Moss, U.S.A., 1917.
True Barber, The, Jörg D'Bombá, East Germany.
Tulips Shall Grow, George Pal, U.S.A., *ca.* 1942.
Two Balls Of Wool, Hermína Týrlová, Czech., 1962.
Two Dorothys, The, Zenon Wasilewski, Poland, 1955.
Two Frosts, The, (cartoon and puppet), Jiří Trnka, Czech., 1954.
Two Gun Rusty, George Pal, U.S.A., 1944.
Two Lamps, Tadeusz Wilkosz, Poland, 1962.
Ugly Cockroach, The, Edward Sturlis, Poland, 1961.
Unbelievable Story, An, Kurt Weiler, East Germany.
Uniform, The, Edward Sturlis, Poland, 1966.
Uninvited Guest, The, Teresa Badzian, Poland, *ca.* 1960.
Utica Club Beer Commercials (60), Louis Bunin, U.S.A., *ca.* 1968.
Valiant Hans, Klaus Georgi and Katja Georgi, East Germany.

A scene from Týrlová's TAMING OF THE DRAGON (reproduced from Tenčik's Hermína Týrlová).

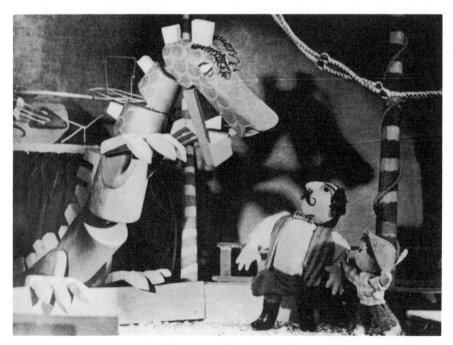

Voice Of the Nightingale, The, Ladislas Starevitch, France, 1923.
We Build a School, Jörg D'Bombá, East Germany, 1961.
Western, Günter Rätz, East Germany, 1965.
Western Daze, George Pal, U.S.A., 1941.
What Ho, She Bumps!, George Pal, Great Britain, 1937.
What Is Lacking? (cartoon and puppet), Hermína Týrlová, Czech., 1947.
What the Moon Saw, B. Haupe and H. Bielińska, Poland, 1955.
Whistle, The, Hermína Týrlová, Czech., 1970.
Who Owns the Acorns?, Rasa Strautman, U.S.S.R., 1966.
Wilber the Lion, George Pal, U.S.A., *ca.* 1944.
Wolf and the Seven Children, The, Nemolayev, U.S.S.R.
Wonder-Working Doctor, The, Kurt Herbert Schulz, East Germany.
Wooden Athletes, The, Charles Urban, Great Britain, 1912.
Wooden Horseman, The, Zenon Wasilewski, Poland, 1965.
Woolly Tale, The, Hermína Týrlová, Czech., 1964.
World In Opera, The, Jerzy Kotowski, Poland, 1969.
Ziegfeld Follies Prologue, The, Louis Bunin, U.S.A., 1948.
Zinzabelle In Paris, Ladislas Starevitch (with Sonika Bo), France, 1949.

CHRONOLOGICAL
FILMOGRAPHY OF PUPPET FILMS

1907
The Haunted Hotel (object animation), James Stuart Blackton, U.S.A.
1908
Dreams of Toyland, Arthur Melbourne Cooper, Great Britain.
Noah's Ark, Arthur Melbourne Cooper, Great Britain.
Paper Cock-A-Doodle (trick film with cut-out paper birds), Pathé Brothers, France.
1910
The Automatic Moving Company (*Mobelier fidèle*), Emile Cohl, France.
Le petit Faust, Emile Cohl, France.
1911
The Grasshopper and the Ant, Ladislas Starevitch, Russia.
The Stag-Beetles, Ladislas Starevitch, Russia.
A Tragedy In Toyland, Kalem Company, U.S.A.
1912
The Birth Of the Hosts Of the Forest, Ladislas Starevitch, Russia.
Flying Insects, Ladislas Starevitch, Russia.
Happy Scenes In the Lives Of the Animals, Ladislas Starevitch, Russia.
Revenge Of the Kinematographic Cameraman, Ladislas Starevitch, Russia.
The Wooden Athletes, Charles Urban, Great Britain.
1917
The Dinosaur and the Missing Link, Willis H. O'Brien, U.S.A.
Dolly Doings, Howard S. Moss, U.S.A.

Dunkling Of the Circus, Howard S. Moss, U.S.A.
Goldilocks and the Three Bears, Howard S. Moss, U.S.A.
In the Jungle, Howard S. Moss, U.S.A.
Jimmy Gets the Pennant, Howard S. Moss, U.S.A.
A Kitchen Romance, Howard S. Moss, U.S.A.
The Magic Pig, Howard S. Moss, U.S.A.
Midnight Frolic, Howard S. Moss, U.S.A.
Out In the Rain, Howard S. Moss, U.S.A.
Prehistoric Poultry: The Dinornis Or the Great Roaring Whiffenpoof, Willis
    O'Brien, U.S.A.
R.F.D. 1000 B.C., Willis H. O'Brien, U.S.A.
School Days, Howard S. Moss, U.S.A.
A Trip To the Moon, Howard S. Moss, U.S.A.
1919
Story Of a Little Girl Who Wanted To Be, Ladislas Starevitch, France.
1920
The Marriage Of Babylas, Ladislas Starevitch, France.
1921
The Scarecrow, Ladislas Starevitch, France.
1923
The Frogs Who Wanted a King, Ladislas Starevitch, France.
The Little Street-Singer, Ladislas Starevitch, France.
The Voice Of the Nightingale, Ladislas Starevitch.
1924
The Claws Of the Spider, Ladislas Starevitch, France.
Cracked Ice, Edwin Miles Fadman, U.S.A.
Mose and Funny Face Make Angel Cake, Edwin Miles Fadman, U.S.A.
1927
Black Love and White Love, Ladislas Starevitch, France.
The City Rat and the Country Rat, Ladislas Starevitch, France.
The Eyes Of the Dragon, Ladislas Starevitch, France.
1928
Eva and the Grasshopper, Diehl Brothers, Germany.
The Magic Clock, Ladislas Starevitch, France.
The Queen Of the Butterflies, Ladislas Starevitch, France.
Toyland Topics, Great Britain.
1929
The Tale Of the Fox, Ladislas Starevitch, France.
The Petite Parade, Ladislas Starevitch, France.
1930
The Card Maniac, Richard Teschner, Austria.
The Lion and the Gnat, Ladislas Starevitch, France.
1931
The Bed Bug, A. Ptushko, U.S.S.R.
"Bratishkin" series, A. Ptushko, U.S.S.R.
Play and Work, A. Ptushko, U.S.S.R.
1932
Midnight, George Pal, Germany.
The Old Lion, Ladislas Starevitch, France.

1933

Coster Bill Of Paris (puppet sequence by Starevitch), Jacque De Baroncelli, France.

"Experimental Animation," Len Lye, Great Britain.

The Ringmaster, Ladislas Starevitch, France.

1934

All Quiet In the East, P. Bianchi, France.

The Mascot, Ladislas Starevitch, France.

The Navigator, Ladislas Starevitch, France.

The Revolution Of the Bulb, George Pal, Holland.

1935

Cupid's Arrow, Ladislas Starevitch, France.

Ether Ship, George Pal, Holland.

In the Land Of the Vampires, Ladislas Starevitch, France.

The Magic Atlas, George Pal, Holland.

The New Gulliver, A. Ptushko, U.S.S.R.

Sinbad, George Pal, Great Britain.

The Sleeping Beauty, Alexander Alexeieff, France.

1936

The Adventures Of Mr. Pry, Karel Dodal and Hermína Týrlová, Czech.

Aladdin and the Wonderful Lamp, George Pal, Great Britain.

Ali Baba, George Pal, Great Britain.

Birth Of a Robot, Len Lye and Humphrey Jennings, Great Britain.

On Parade, George Pal, Great Britain,

1937

"Alexeieff Advertising Films" (puppets and cartoon for Paris exposition), Alexander Alexeieff, France.

What Ho, She Bumps!, George Pal, Great Britain.

1938

Blue Beard, Jean Painlevé and René Bertrand, France.

The Lantern Mystery, Karel Dodal and Hermína Týrlová, Czech.

Lovers In the South Seas, George Pal, U.S.A.

Puss In Boots, Diehl Brothers, Germany.

The Race Of the Rabbit and the Hedgehog, Diehl Brothers, Germany.

Sky Pirates, George Pal, Great Britain.

1939

The Golden Key, A. Ptushko, U.S.S.R.

Love On the Range, George Pal, Great Britain.

Pete Roleum and His Cousins, Joseph Losey and Howard Bay, U.S.A.

1940

Date With Duke, George Pal, U.S.A.

Dipsy Gypsy, George Pal, U.S.A.

1941

Rhythm In the Ranks, George Pal, U.S.A.

Western Daze, George Pal, U.S.A.

1942

Ferda the Ant, Hermína Týrlová, Czech.

Jasper and the Haunted House, George Pal, U.S.A.

Jasper and the Watermelons, George Pal, U.S.A.

Tulips Shall Grow, George Pal, U.S.A.
1943
Bravo Mr. Strauss, George Pal, U.S.A.
Goodnight Rusty, George Pal, U.S.A.
Jasper and the Choo Choo, George Pal, U.S.A.
Jasper Goes Fishing, George Pal, U.S.A.
Jasper's Music Lesson, George Pal, U.S.A.
1944
And To Think I Saw It On Mulberry Street, George Pal. U.S.A.
Jasper Goes Hunting, George Pal, U.S.A.
Jasper's Paradise, George Pal, U.S.A.
Little Black Sambo, George Pal, U.S.A.
Package For Jasper, George Pal, U.S.A.
Two Gun Rusty, George Pal, U.S.A.
Wilber the Lion, George Pal, U.S.A.
1945
Jasper and the Beanstalk, George Pal, U.S.A.
Jasper Tell, George Pal, U.S.A.
Jasper's Booby Trap, George Pal, U.S.A.
Jasper's Close Shave, George Pal, U.S.A.
Jasper's Minstrels, George Pal, U.S.A.
1946
Christmas Dream, Karel Zeman, Czech.
The Dragon Of Kraków, Zenon Wasilewski, Poland.
The Hamster, Karel Zeman, Czech.
Jasper's Derby, George Pal, U.S.A.
John Henry and the Inky-Poo, George Pal, U.S.A.
Pawel and Gawel, R. Potoci, Poland.
1947
The Czech Year, Jiří Trnka, Czech.
The Harlequin Nimbo, Zenon Wasilewski, Poland.
A Horseshoe For Luck, Karel Zeman, Czech.
Little Soldier, Paul Grimault, France.
Lullaby, Hermína Týrlová, Czech.
Mr. Plume Has a Dream, Zenon Wasilewski, Poland.
Mr. Prokouk and Red Tape, Karel Zeman, Czech.
Mr. Prokouk's Temptation, Karel Zeman, Czech.
Revolt Of the Toys, Hermína Týrlová, Czech.
The Times of King Krakus, Zenon Wasilewski, Poland.
What Is Lacking? (cartoon and puppet), Hermína Týrlová, Czech.
1948
An Accident (puppet with live actors), Hermína Týrlová, Czech.
Berceuse, Hermína Týrlová, Czech.
The Emperor's Nightingale, Jiří Trnka, Czech.
Mr. Prokouk Inventor, Karel Zeman, Czech.
Mr. Prokouk On a Brigade, Karel Zeman, Czech.
The Ziegfeld Follies Prologue, Louis Bunin, U.S.A.
1949
Inspiration, Karel Zeman, Czech.

Song Of the Prairie, Jiří Trnka, Czech.
The Story Of the Double-Bass, Jiří Trnka, Czech.
Zinzabelle In Paris, Ladislas Starevitch (with Sonika Bo), France.
1950
Fern Flowers, Ladislas Starevitch (with Sonika Bo), France.
King Lavra, Karel Zeman, Czech.
The Misfit Figure, Hermína Týrlová, Czech.
A Nocturnal Romance, Hermína Týrlová, Czech.
Prince Bajaja, Jiří Trnka, Czech.
1951
Alice In Wonderland, Louis Bunin, Great Britain.
The Bad Little Fox, Zenon Wasilewski, Poland.
The Devil's Mill, Jiří Trnka, Czech.
The Gingerbread Cottage, Břetislav Pojar, Czech.
The Happy Circus (cut paper), Jiří Trnka, Czech.
The Rascal Snail, Haupe and Bielińska, Poland.
The Stork and the Fox, Zenon Wasilewski, Poland.
1952
The Deceived Fox, Bob Calinecu, Romania.
Kutasek and Kutilka, Jiří Trnka, Czech.
The Nine Chickens, Hermína Týrlová, Czech.
The Orchard Of Père Laurent, Haupe and Bielińska, Poland.
The Treasure Of Bird Island, Karel Zeman, Czech.
1953
A Commune Effort, Olga Totwen, Poland.
Figurehead, Halas and Batchelor, Great Britain.
Janosik, Haupe and Bielińska, Poland.
Old Czech Legends, Jiří Trnka, Czech.
The Taming Of the Dragon, Hermína Týrlová, Czech.
1954
A Commune, Ewa and Olga Totwen, Poland.
A Drop Too Much, Břetislav Pojar, Czech.
The Magic Pencil, Tsin Si, China (?).
Good Soldier Schweik, Jiří Trnka, Czech.
Hansel and Gretel, Michael Myerberg Productions, U.S.A.
The Two Frosts, Jiří Trnka, Czech.
1955
The Boastful Knight, Edward Sturlis, Poland.
Circus Hurvinek, Jiří Trnka, Czech.
Courting Songs, Louis Bunin, U.S.A.
Garland Of Folk Songs, Hermína Týrlová, Czech.
Goldilocks, Hermína Týrlová, Czech.
Gumbasia, Art Clokey, U.S.A.
The Little Boy Doesn't Wash, Edward Sturlis, Poland.
Mr. Prokouk, Animal Fancier, Karel Zeman, Czech.
The New House, Teresa Badzian, Poland.
Olde Bangum, Louis Bunin, U.S.A.
The Story Of Michalkowice, Zenon Wasilewski, Poland.
The Strange Voyage, Teresa Badzian, Poland.

The Two Dorothys, Zenon Wasilewski, Poland.
What the Moon Saw, Haupe and Bielińska, Poland.
1956
Alsort Ballet, J. Barton, Great Britain.
The Barrel-Organ, Haupe and Bielińska, Poland.
The Magic Gift, Zenon Wasilewski, Poland.
Misha the Ball, Hermína Týrlová, Czech.
The Puppet Parade, Hermína Týrlová, Czech.
1957
Folksong Fantasy, Alma Duncan, Canada.
Go East, Young Woman, J. Barton, Great Britain.
Lazy Martin, Hermína Týrlová, Czech.
Mr. Prokouk, Detective, Karel Zeman, Czech.
Negrita's Island, Gheorghe Sibianu, Romania.
1958
The Emperor's New Clothes, Kurt Herbert Schulz, East Germany.
Homer, the Horse Who Couldn't Talk, Louis Bunin, U.S.A.
The Knot In the Handkerchief, Hermína Týrlová, Czech.
Kumak the Sleepy Hunter, Alma Duncan, Canada.
The Lion and the Song, Břetislav Pojar, Czech.
The Little Umbrella, Břetislav Pojar, Czech.
The Magic Box, Stefan Topalogikov, Bulgaria.
Midnight Incident, Břetislav Pojar, Czech.
The Puppet's Dream, Al Sens, Canada.
Romeo and Juliet, Hermína Týrlová, Czech.
The Secret Way, Herbert K. Schulz, East Germany.
Speijbl On the Track, Břetislav Pojar, Czech.
The Swineherd, Hermína Týrlová, Czech.
Teddy Brumm, Günter Rätz, East Germany.
The Ape, Yang Tei, China (?).
1959
Changing Of the Guard, Haupe and Belińska, Poland.
Mr. Prokouk In the Circus, Karel Zeman, Czech.
The Devil's Valley, Katja Georgi, East Germany.
The Little Train, Hermína Týrlová, Czech.
The Lost Doll, Hermína Týrlová, Czech.
A Midsummer Nights Dream, Jiří Trnka, Czech.
Noah's Ark, Disney Studio, U.S.A.
The Princess and the Pea, Katja Georgi, East Germany.
1960
The Barrel-Organ, J. Kotowski, Poland.
Cactus, L. Dembinski, Poland.
The Ghost Can't Take It, Lidia Hornicka, Poland.
Hats Down!, Stefan Topalogikov, Bulgaria.
The King Of the Animals, Günter Rätz, East Germany.
Lajkonik, M. Kruger, Poland.
A Lesson, Hermína Týrlová, Czech.
The Little Giraffe, Teresa Badzian, Poland.
The Little Pig, Zenon Wasilewski, Poland.

From Trnka's THE CYBERNETIC GRANDMOTHER (photo courtesy of Ceskoslovenský Filmexport).

The Magic Hoe, Stefan Topalogikov, Bulgaria.
Manguar, Edward Sturlis, Poland.
Mr. Elephant, Teresa Badzian, Poland.
Mr. Lens and the Wilderness, J. Kotowski, Poland.
Never Tease a Lion, T. Wilkosz, Poland.
One Little Indian, Alma Duncan, Canada.
Rhapsody In Wood, Bob Calinescu, Romania.
Song Of the Dove, Günter Rätz, East Germany.
The Thieves, W. Kondek, Poland.
The Travelling Tune, Joop Geesink, Holland.
The Uninvited Guest, Teresa Badzian, Poland.
1961
Course For Husbands, Vladimir Lehky, Czech.
The Happy Man, Stefan Topalogikov, Bulgaria.
The Inquisitive Letter, Hermína Týrlová, Czech.
The Pyramid, Katja Georgi, East Germany.
The Ugly Cockroach, Edward Sturlis, Poland.
We Build a School, Jörg D'Bombá, East Germany.
1962
About Johnny Who Made Shoes For Dogs, Lidia Hornicka, Poland.
Adventures Of An Alarm-Clock, Jania Hartwig, Poland.
The Basilisk, L. Serafinowicz and W. Wieczorkieloica, Poland.
The Bath House, Yutkevich and Karanovich, U.S.S.R.
The Black King, Jerzy Kotowski, Poland.
Course For Wives, Vladimir Lehký, Czech.

The Crime On Cat-the-Ventriloquist Street, Zenon Wasilewski, Poland.
The Devil's Dirty Work, Jörg D'Bombá, East Germany.
The Dingo Dog and the Kangaroo, Louis Bunin, U.S.A.
Joseph and His Brethren, Israel.
The King's Sentence, Katarzyna Latałło, Poland.
Little Kate, Hermína Týrlová, Czech.
Little Music, Teresa Badzian, Poland.
Matches, Katja Georgi, East Germany.
The Naughty Chicken, Stefan Topalogikov, Bulgaria.
Orpheus and Eurydice, Edward Sturlis, Poland.
The Passion, Jiří Trnka, Czech.
Plumbers, Zofia Wdowkówna-Oldak, Poland.
The Tea-Pot, Haupe and Bielińska, Poland.
Two Balls of Wool, Hermína Týrlová, Czech.
Two Lamps, Tadeusz Wilkosz, Poland.
1963
A Cat's Word Of Honor, Břetislav Pojar, Czech.
The Cybernetic Grandmother, Jiří Trnka, Czech.
Drawing For Cats, Břetislav Pojar, Czech.
Lake Of the Fairies, Gheorghe Sibianu, Romania.
The Marble, Hermína Týrlová, Czech.
Musicians, Katja Georgi, East Germany.
School For Cats, Břetislav Pojar, Czech.
1964
Billiards, Břetislav Pojar, Czech.
Clay, Elliot Noyse, U.S.A.
The Introductory Speech Is By . . . , Břetislav Pojar, Czech.
Philips Cavalcade, Joop Geesink, Holland.
Plastic In the Park, Katja Georgi, East Germany.
A Scrap Of Paper and a Piece Of String, John Korty.
The Three Heros, Stefan Topalogikov, Bulgaria.
The Woolly Tale, Hermína Týrlová, Czech.
1965
Adventures In a Cupboard, Edward Sturlis, Poland.
Alarm, Teresa Badzian, Poland.
The Apostle, Günter Rätz, East Germany.
Archangel Gabriel and Mother Goose, Jiří Trnka, Czech.
The Button, Teresa Badzian, Poland.
Cats and Kittens, Tadeusz Wilkosz, Poland.
Come and Play, Sir (series of three), Břetislav Pojar, Czech.
Concurrence, Katja Georgi, East Germany.
Congratulations, Günter Rätz, East Germany.
The Enchanted Wampum, Lidia Hornicka, Poland.
Escape, Lucjan Debiński, Poland.
Good Day Mr. H., Katja Georgi, East Germany.
The Hand, Jiří Trnka, Czech.
A Honeycomb, Jerzy Kotowski, Poland.
Ideal, Břetislav Pojar, Czech.
Kids On a Belfry, Jania Hartwig, Poland.

From *A STUDY IN PAPER (1965), by the author (photo by L. Bruce Holman).*

Noise, Zofia Wdowkowna-Oldak, Poland.
The Orator, Břetislav Pojar, Czech.
Photography, Günter Rätz, East Germany.
Romance, Břetislav Pojar, Czech.
Shadow Of Time, Jerzy Kotowski, Poland.
Stone and Life, Garik Seko, Czech.
Study In Paper, L. Bruce Holman, U.S.A.
Swan Lake, Stefan Topalogikov, Bulgaria.
Western, Güntar Rätz, East Germany.
The Wooden Horseman, Zenon Wasilewski, Poland.
1966
At the End Of the Road, Wang Chou-Tchez, China.
Aviation, Günter Rätz, East Germany.
The Blue Pinafore, Hermína Týrlová, Czech.
The Boy Or the Girl, Hermína Týrlová, Czech.
The Cock, Lucjan Dembiński, Poland.
Curiosity, Günter Rätz, East Germany.
The Fairy Ring, Tadeusz Wilkosz, Poland.
For Pete's Sake, Lidia Hornicka, Poland.
Katherine and the Hangman, Katarzyna Latałło, Poland.
Little Bear's Journey, Rasa Strautman, U.S.S.R.
A Little Quartet, Edward Sturlis, Poland.
A Night Of Surprises, Jania Hartwig, Poland.
The Place, Edward Sturlis, Poland.

The Precursor, Zofia Wdowkówna-Oldak, Poland.
Small Banknote, Wacław Krukowski, Poland.
Snowman, Hermína Týrlová, Czech.
The Surprise, Teresa Badzian, Poland.
The Tiny Tot, Lucjan Dembiński, Poland.
The Uniform, Edward Sturlis, Poland.
Who Owns the Acorns?, Rasa Strautman, U.S.S.R.
1967
About a Comb Who Didn't Want To Brush His Teeth, Poland.
About Bachtalo, the Gypsy, K. Dobrowolska, Poland.
Anton the Musician, Günter Rätz, East Germany.
The Blue Duckling, Lucjan Dembiński, Poland.
The Demon, Lucjan Dembiński, Poland.
Dogs Heaven, Hermína Týrlová, Czech.
A Game, Teresa Badzian, Poland.
Hold Your Hats, Břetislav Pojar, Czech.
The Little Kangaroo, Teresa Badzian, Poland.
A Man From the Mirror, Zenon Wasilewski, Poland.
The Miraculous Spring, Edward Sturlis, Poland.
The Peacock Princess, People's Republic of China.
Philips On Parade, Joop Geesink, Holland.
The Sack, Tadeusz Wilkosz, Poland.
The Shah's Magic Beard, Bogdan Nowicki, Poland.
Spaarroussel, Joop Geesink, Holland.
The Tangle, K. Latałło and W. Antosik, Poland.
The Thorn, Katja Georgi, East Germany.
Three Wishes, Günter Rätz, East Germany.
1968
Christmas Sonnet, Hermína Týrlová, Czech.
The Christmas Tree, Hermína Týrlová, Czech.
Duet, Vladimir Lehký, Czech.
Ferko the Pouch, Hermína Týrlová, Czech.
Human Foolishness, G. Sibianu, Romania.
It's Hard To Recognise a Princess, Břetislav Pojar, Czech.
The Little Bead Fish, Hermína Týrlová, Czech.
Mr. Servadac's Ark, Karel Zeman, Czech.
To See Or Not To See, Břetislav Pojar, Czech.
Utica Club Beer Commercials (60), Louis Bunin, U.S.A.
1969
Bill Has a Hundred Faces, István Imre, Hungary.
Breaking Of Branches Is Forbidden, Kihachiro Kawamoto, Japan.
The Cat and the Sphinx, Louis Bunin, U.S.A.
Der Gardinentraum (Curtain-Dream), Katja Georgi and Heinrich-Greif-Preis-
        tragger, East Germany.
Matrioska, Co Hoedeman, Canada.
The Musical Box, Jerzy Kotowski, Poland.
Oddball, Co Hoedeman, Canada.
The Selfish Giant, David Allen, U.S.A.
Stairs, Stefan Schabenbeck, Poland.

Half-round figures created on a sheet of glass by Hermína Týrlová (photo courtesy of Ceskoslovenský Filmexport).

The Star Of Bethlehem, Hermína Týrlová, Czech.
The World In Opera, Jerzy Kotowski, Poland.
1970
The Crooked Chimney, Pavel Prochazka, Czech.
Cubes Ole, Richard Thomas, U.S.A.
East, West, Home Is Best, Josef Kluge, Czech.
It's a Fiasco, Gentlemen, Břetislav Pojar and Miroslav Stephanek, Czech.
The Meeting, Jana Olexová, Czech.
Painting, Hermína Týrlová, Czech.
Scissors, František Vystrčil, Czech.
The Sculptress Of Policka, Jaroslav Boček, Czech.
The Whistle, Hermína Týrlová, Czech.

From Trnka's THE HAND (photo courtesy of Československý Filmexport).

EIGHT LEADING PUPPET ANIMATORS

GEORGE PAL (1908–   ) [Germany, Holland, Great Britain, and U.S.A.]
ca. 1932 *Midnight* (for a Berlin cigarette company).
1933–1935 *The Revolution Of the Bulb* (cartoon for Philips Radio).
1935 *Ether Ship* (for Philips).
　　The Magic Atlas (for Philips).
　　Sinbad.
1936 *Aladdin and the Wonderful Lamp.*
　　Ali Baba.
　　On Parade (for Horlick's Malted Milk).
1937 *What Ho! She Bumps* (for Horlick's).
1938 *Lovers In the South Seas.*
　　Sky Pirates.
1939 *Love On the Range.*
1940 *Dipsy Gypsy.*
ca. 1940–1949 *Date With Duke.*
　　Gooseberry Pie.
1941 *Rhythm In the Ranks.*
　　Western Daze.
1942 *Jasper and the Haunted House.*
　　Jasper and the Watermelons.
　　Tulips Shall Grow.

1943 *Bravo Mr. Strauss.*
    Goodnight Rusty.
    Five Hundred Hats Of Bartholomew Cubbins.
    Jasper and the Choo Choo.
    Jasper Goes Fishing.
    Jasper's Music Lesson.
1944 *And To Think I Saw It On Mulberry Street.*
    Jasper Goes Hunting.
    Jasper's Paradise.
    Package For Jasper.
    Two Gun Rusty.
ca. 1944 *Little Black Sambo.*
    Wilber the Lion.
1945 *Jasper and the Beanstalk.*
    Jasper's Booby Trap.
    Jasper's Close Shave.
    Jasper's Minstrels.
    Jasper Tell.
1946 *Jasper's Derby.*
    John Henry and the Inky Poo.

BRETISLAV POJAR (1923–   )   [Czechoslovakia]
1951 *The Gingerbread Cottage* (puppets by Trnka).
1954 *A Drop Too Much.*
    The Gold Bay Adventure (live-action).
1958 *The Little Umbrella.*
    Speijbl On the Track.
ca. 1958–1962 *Bombomania* (cartoon).
    How To Furnish a Flat (mixed media).
    The Lion and the Song.
    Midnight Incident.
1963 *A Cat's World Of Honour* (cut paper).
    Drawing For Cats (cut paper).
    School For Cats (cut paper).
1964 *Billiards.*
    The Introductory Speech Is By . . .
1965 *Ideal.*
    Orator.
    Romance.
1965–1967 *Come and Play, Sir* (series of three).
1967 *Hold Your Hats.*
1968 *It's Hard To Recognise a Princess.*
    To See Or Not To See.
1970 *It's a Fiasco, Gentlemen.*

LADISLAS STAREVITCH (6 Aug. 1892–1965)   [Russia and France]
There is no consensus regarding either the number of films made by Starevitch
or their production dates. Many were re-edited and released with new titles. The
following list is believed to be accurate regarding titles and dates, although it

is not a complete filmography. In instances where the English title is other than a literal translation, the French title is given, since most of Starevitch's films are better-known by the latter.

ca. 1911 *The Stag-Beetles* (*Le plus beau des lucannes, Le cerf-volant,* [Russian] *Prekrasnaya lyukanida*).

1911 *The Grasshopper and the Ant.*

ca. 1912 *The Birth Of the Host Of the Forest.*
Happy Scenes In the Life Of the Animals.
The Revenge Of a Kinographic Cameraman.

ca. 1913–1915 *Eros and Psyche* (live-action).
The Fisherman and the Little Fish (live-action).
The Four Devils (live-action [a parody of a film by R. Dinesen]).
Jola (live-action).
The Night Of Christmas (live-action, after a story by Gogol).
Pan Twardowsky (live-action).
Ruslan and Ludmila (live-action, after Pushkin).
Sniegourochka (live-action).
Stella Maris (live-action).
Terrible Vengeance (live-action).
Wij (live-action, after Gogol).

ca. 1920 *The Marriage Of Babylas.*

1921 *The Scarecrow.*

1923 *The Frogs Who Wanted a King.*
The Little Street-Singer.
The Voice Of the Nightingale.

1924 *In the Claws Of the Spider.*

From the COME AND PLAY, SIR series by Bretislav Pojar (photo courtesy of Ceskslovenský Filmexport).

1927 *The City Rat and the Country Rat.*
      The Eyes Of the Dragon.
ca. 1927 *Black Love and White Love.*
1928 *The Magic Clock.*
ca. 1928 *The Queen Of the Butterflies.*
1929 *The Petite Parade.*
1929–1939 *The Tale Of the Fox.*
ca. 1930 *The Lion and the Gnat.*
1932 *The Old Lion* (*Le lion devenu vieux*).
1933 Puppet sequence for *Coster Bill Of Paris.*
ca. 1933 *The Ringmaster.*
1934 *The Mascot* (*Fetiche mascotte,* also *Duffy Mascot*).
      The Navigator.
1935 *In the Land Of the Vampires.*
ca. 1935 *Cupid's Arrow.*
1949 *Zinzabelle In Paris* (in collaboration with Sonika Bo).
1950 *Fern Flowers* (with Sonika Bo).

JIRÍ TRNKA (1912–Dec. 1969)   [Czechoslovakia]
1945 *Grandpa Planted a Beet* (cartoon).
1946 *The Animals and the Brigands* (cartoon).
      The Chimney Sweep (cartoon [also called *The Devil On Springs, Springer and the SS Men,* and *Spring-heel Jack*]).
      The Gift (cartoon).
1947 *The Czech Year.*
1948 *The Emperor's Nightingale.*
1949 *The Song Of the Prairie.*
      The Story Of the Double-Bass.
1950 *Prince Bayaya.*
1951 *The Devil's Mill.*
      The Golden Fish (cartoon).
      The Happy Circus (cut paper).
1952 *How Grandpa Changed Until Nothing Was Left* (cartoon).
      Kutasek and Kutilka.
1953 *Old Czech Legends.*
1954 *Good Soldier Schweik.*
      The Two Frosts (cartoon and puppet).
1955 *Circus Hurvinek.*
1959 *A Midsummer Night's Dream.*
1962 *The Passion* (also called *Obsession*).
1963 *The Cybernetic Grandmother.*
1965 *Archangel Gabriel and Mother Goose.*
      The Hand.

HERMÍNA TYRLOVÁ (1900–   )   [Czechoslovakia]
1928 *Amorous Water Sprite* (cartoon).
1936 *Adventures Of Mr. Pry* (cartoon and puppet in collaboration with Karel Dodal).
1938 *The Lantern Mystery* (with Karel Dodal).

From *PAINTING (1970)*, by *Hermína Týrlová (photo courtesy of Ceskoslovenský Filmexport)*.

1942 *Ferda the Ant.*
1947 *Lullaby.*
    Revolt Of the Toys.
    What Is Lacking? (cartoon and puppet).
1948 *An Accident* (puppet with live actors).
    Berceuse.
1949 *A Nocturnal Romance.*
1950 *The Misfit Figure.*
1952 *The Nine Chickens.*
1953 *The Taming Of the Dragon.*
1955 *A Garland Of Folk-Songs.*
    Goldilocks.
1956 *Misha the Ball.*
    The Puppet Parade.
1957 *Lazy Martin.*
1958 *The Knot In the Handkerchief.*
    The Swineherd.
1959 *The Little Train.*
    The Lost Doll.
1960 *A Lesson.*
1961 *The Inquisitive Letter.*
1962 *Little Kate.*
    Two Balls Of Wool.

1963 *The Marble.*
1964 *A Woolly Tale.*
1966 *The Blue Pinafore.*
       The Boy Or the Girl.
       Snowman.
1967 *Dog's Heaven.*
1968 *Christmas Sonnet.*
       Christmas Tree.
       Ferko the Pouch.
       The Little Bead Fish.
1969 *The Star Of Bethlehem.*
1970 *Painting.*
       The Whistle.

ZENON WASILEWSKI (–1966)   [Poland]
1946 *The Dragon Of Kraków.*
1947 *The Times Of King Krakus.*
ca. 1947–1950 *The Harlequin Nimbo.*
       Mr. Plume Has a Dream.
1951 *The Bad Little Fox.*
       The Stork and the Fox.
1955 *The Story Of Michalkowice.*
       The Two Dorothys.
1956 *The Magic Gift.*
1960 *The Little Pig.*
1962 *The Crime On Cat-the-Ventriloquist Street.*
1965 *The Wooden Horseman.*
1967 *A Man From the Mirror.*

(Dates not known)
       The Donkey Prince.
       The Gingerbread Kingdom.
       The Princess and the Dragon.

KAREL ZEMAN (3 Nov. 1910–   )   [Czechoslovakia]
1946 *Christmas Dream.*
       The Hamster.
1947 *A Horseshoe For Luck.*
       Mr. Prokouk and the Red Tape (Mr. Prokouk Bureaucrat).
       Mr. Prokouk's Temptation.
1948 *Mr. Prokouk, Inventor.*
       Mr. Prokouk On a Brigade.
1949 *Inspiration.*
1950 *King Lavra.*
1952 *The Treasure Of Bird Island.*
1955 *Journey Into Prehistory* (live action with special effects).
       Mr. Prokouk, Animal Fancier.
1957 *Mr. Prokouk, Detective.*
1958 *An Invention For Destruction* (live action with special effects).

1959 *Mr. Prokouk In the Circus.*
1961 *Baron Munchhausen* (live-action with special effects).
1964 *A Jester's Tale* (live-action with special effects).
1967 *The Stolen Airship* (live-action with special effects).
1968 *Mr. Servadac's Ark.*

Max Kevris inspecting a model rocket-car (photo by the writer).

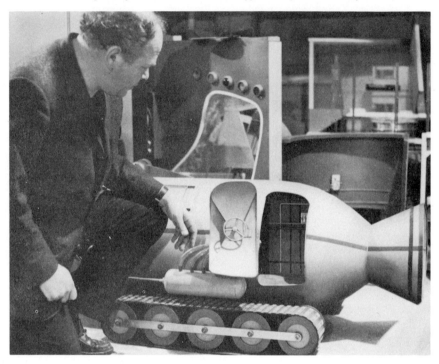

NOTES

1 Bil Baird, "The Art of the Puppet" (New York: Macmillan Co., 1965).

2 Hugo Münsterberg suggested that the persistence of vision is not the mechanism by which motion is perceived from a series of still pictures. Instead, he postulated a phenomenon approximating a mental set for the perception of motion—a "perceptual momentum," which when activated by the progressively-changing pictures tends to carry the impression of motion onward. Later experimenters termed this the "phi phenomenon."—Hugo Münsterberg, "The Film: A Psychological Study" (New York: Dover Pub., 1970), pp. 25–29.

3 Bertrand Russell, "A History of Western Philosophy" (New York: Simon and Schuster, 1945), pp. 804–5.

4 A comprehensive source of information regarding early development of films is C. W. Ceram's "Archaeology of the Cinema" (New York: Harcourt Brace, and World, 1965).

5 A Frenchman, Aimé Augustin, patented an almost identical device in the same year. Others followed rapidly. See Ceram, *ibid*, p. 142.

6 There is disagreement regarding the production date of *Le petit Faust:* the earliest suggested is 1908, but 1910 or 1911 are more probable as Cohl was engaged in cartoon animation during 1908 and 1909 (A. P. Richard, 'Emile Cohl,' "Technique et Material," December 31, 1937).

7 The British Film Institute, "National Film Archive Catalogue" (London: The British Film Institute, 1966), vol. III, p. 182.

8 Ladislas Starevitch, quoted in H. Potamkin's 'Dolls in Motion: Starevitch Reveals Secrets,' "World Film News," April, 1936.

9 *ibid.*

10 'Motion Picture Comedies in Clay,' "Scientific American," vol. CXV (December 16, 1916), p. 553.

11 R. H. Moulton, 'Toyland in the Films,' "Scientific American," vol. CXVII, no. 26 (December 29, 1917).

12 Advertisements for Mo-Toy Comedies may be found in 1917 editions of "The Moving Picture World" magazines.

13 Interview with John Halas, London, December 15, 1970.

14 Ralph Stevenson, "Animation in the Cinema" (London: A Zwemmer, 1965; new and revised edition, Tantivy Press, 1973), p. 93.

15 Hermína Týrlová, quoted in Vlasta Jablonská, "Hermína Týrlová" (Prague: Československý Filmexport, 1970), p. 2.

16 Stephenson, *op. cit.,* p. 93.

17 Interview with Dr. Marie Benešová, Prague, December 30, 1970.

18 Trnka's career and his films are described at length in Jaroslav Boček's "Jiří Trnka, Artist and Puppet Master" (Prague: Artia, 1965); material is presently being gathered for a second book.

19 Interview with B. Pojar, Prague, December 29, 1970.

20 Marie Benešová (ed.), "Czechoslovak Films for Children" (Prague: Central Film Distribution in co-operation with the Czech Film Institute, 1965).

21 Stephenson, *op. cit.,* p. 118.

[22] Marshall McLuhan, an address at Syracuse University, 1970.

[23] Quoted in John Halas and Roger Manvell's "Art in Movement" (New York: Hastings House, 1970), p. 42.

[24] Eadweard Muybridge's studies of human motion are helpful in this—"The Human Figure in Motion" (New York: Dover Pub., 1955).

[25] This process is described in an article by David Allen— 'David Allen's Models,' "Ready for Showing," vol. 1, no. 1 (1965), p. 28.

[26] Interview with Louis Bunin, November 5, 1970.

[27] Quoted in Halas and Manvell, "The Technique of Film Animation," p. 264.

[28] A. Ptushko, 'The Coming of a New Gulliver,' "Sight and Sound," Summer, 1935.

[29] B. Pojar, "Content of a Speech by Bretislav Pojar" (from a typed copy of an address delivered to the Royal Photographic Society, London, 1963).

[30] Systems for calibrating movements may be found in Roy P. Madsen's "Animated Film" (New York: Interland, 1969), pp. 69–70.

[31] For an explanation of front-screen projection, see 'Front-Screen Projection,' "Aperture," **XXX**, 2, Feb., 1970.

[32] Interview with Co Hoedeman, Montreal, January 12, 1971.

[33] A. Ptushko, *op. cit.*

[34] S. Kracauer, "Theory of Film" (New York: Oxford University Press, 1960), p. 12.

[35] Quoted by Halas and Manvell, "The Technique of Film Animation," p. 264.

BIBLIOGRAPHY

Books

Aaronson, Charles S. (ed.). *International Motion Picture Almanac.* New York: Quigley Publications, 1962.

Adamec, Oldřich, and Benešová, Marie (eds.). *Czechoslovak Film Annual: Cartoon and Puppet Films.* Prague: Československý Filmexport, 1966.

Adamec, Oldřich (ed.). *Czechoslovak Short Film 1962–1963.* Prague: Czechoslovak Film Institute, 1963.

Adamec, Oldřich (ed.). *Czechoslovak Film Annual 1965.* Prague: Československý Filmexport, 1956.

Alberti, Walter. *Il Cinema di Animazione.* Torino: Edizioni Radio Italiana, 1957.

Arnheim, Rudolf. *Art and Visual Perception: A Psychology of the Creative Eye.* Berkeley and Los Angeles: University of California Press, 1965.

Association Internationale du Film d'Animation. *Animation 1962.* (Publication of the Festival at Annecy, 1962.)

Baird, Bil. *The Art of the Puppet.* New York: Macmillan Co., 1965.

Barton, J. *Animating for Fun and Analysis of the Species.* London: Stockbook Co., 1957.

Bazin, André. *What Is Cinema?* Berkeley and Los Angeles: University of California Press, 1970.

Beaumont, Cyril. *Puppets and Puppetry.* London and New York: The Studio Publications, 1958.

Benayoun, Robert. *Le Dessin Animé après Walt Disney.* Paris: Societé Francaise des Presses Suisses, 1961.

Benešová, Marie; *Czechoslovak Films for Children.* Prague: Central Film Distribution and the Film Institute of Czechoslovak Film, 1965.

Boček, Jaroslav. *Jiří Trnka, Artist and Puppet Master,* 1st Eng. Ed. Prague: Artia, 1965.

Boussinot, Roger (ed.). *L'Encyclopédie du Cinéma.* Paris: Bordas, 1967.

The British Film Institute. *National Film Archive Catalogue,* vol. III. London: 1966.

Ceram, C. W. [Kurt W. Marek]. *Archaeology of the Cinema.* New York: Harcourt, Brace, and World, 1965.

Československý Filmexport. *The Czechoslovak Films for Children and Youth.* Prague: 1969.

Český Filmovy Ustav. *Hermína Týrlová.* Prague: 1970.

Československý Státni Film. *Panorama of Puppet Films.* Prague: *ca.* 1957.

113

Cinémathèque de Belgique. *Le Dessin Animé.* (Publication of the Exposition Organisée par la Cinémathèque de Belgique) 1946. ·

Cinémathèque Canadienne. *Exposition Mondial du Cinema d'Animation.* (Catalogue of a film exhibition at Sir George Williams University) Montreal: 1967.

Cowie, Peter (ed.). *International Film Guide* (Annual editions, 1964 onwards). London: Tantivy.

Dayborn, John. *The Animated Cartoon.* Fountain Movie Book.

DEFA-Aussenhandel. *Trickfilme.* (Catalogue of DEFA-Aussenhandel Studios). Berlin: *ca.* 1965.

Dickinson, Thorold, and De La Roche, Catherine. *Soviet Cinema.* London: The Falcon Press, 1948.

Durgnat, Raymond. *Films and Feelings.* Cambridge, Mass.: The M.I.T. Press, 1967.

Eastman Kodak Company. *Basic Titling and Animation for Motion Pictures,* 2nd ed. Rochester: 1970.

Esnault, Philippe. *Chronologie du Cinéma Mondial.* Paris: Les Grand Films Classiques, 1963.

Fescourt, Henri (ed.). *Le Cinéma: Des Origines à Nos Jours.* Paris: Les Editions du Cygne, 1932.

Galerie Hořejš. *Jiří Trnka,* (Catalogue of an exhibition of paintings and lithographs by Jiří Trnka at the Galerie Hořejš, Prague. Undated.).

Ginzburg, S. *The Animated and Puppet Film: Outline of the Development of Soviet Cartoon Cinematography (Risovanny i kukolny film).* Moscow: State Press (Iskusstvo), 1957. (Filmography only.)

Halas, John (text), and Herdeg, Walter (ed.). *Film and TV Graphics.* Zurich: Graphis Press, New York: Hastings House, 1957.

Halas, John, and Manvell, Roger. *Art in Movement: New Directions in Animation.* New York: Hastings House, 1970–

Halas, John, and Manvell, Roger. *The Technique of Film Animation.* New York: Hastings House, 1963.

Halas, John, and Manvell, Roger. *Design in Motion.* New York: Hastings House, 1962.

Halliwell, Leslie. *The Filmgoer's Companion.* New York: Hill and Wang, 1965.

Hibbins, Nina. *Screen Series: Eastern Europe: An Illustrated Guide.* London: A. Zwemmer; New York: A. S. Barnes, 1969.

Institut des hautes études cinématographiques. *La Cinéma d'Animation dans le Monde.* Paris: 1956.

Jablonská, Vlasta. *Hermína Týrlová.* Prague: Československý Filmexport, 1970.

Kinsey, Anthony. *Animated Film Making.* London: Studio Visual, 1970.

Kracauer, Siegfried. *Theory of Film: The Redemption of Physical Reality.* New York: Oxford University Press, 1960.

Levitan, Eli L. *Animation Art in the Commercial Film.* New York: Reinhold, 1960.

Levitan, Eli L. *Animation Techniques and Commercial Film Production.* New York: Reinhold, 1962.

Madsen, Roy P. *Animated Film: Concepts, Methods, Uses.* New York: Interland, 1969.

Malik, Jan, and Kolar, Erik. *The Puppet Theatre in Czechoslovakia.* Prague: Obis, 1970.

Martin, André. *Family Tree of the Origin and Golden Age of the American Cartoon Film.* Montreal: La Cinémathèque Canadienne, 1967.

Minter, Leonard (ed.). *Ready for Showing,* vol. 1, no. 1, Sweetwater, Texas: 1965.

Mitry, Jean. *Dictionnaire du Cinéma.* Paris: Library LaRousse, 1963.

Münsterberg, Hugo. *The Film: A Psychological Study.* New York: Dover Publications, 1970.

Museum of Modern Art. *A Short History of Animation.* New York: Museum of Modern Art Film Library Publication, 1940.

Muybridge, Eadweard. *Animals in Motion.* New York: Dover Publications. 1957.

Muybridge, Eadweard. *The Human Figure in Motion.* New York: Dover Publications, 1955.

Obraztsov, Sergey. *My Profession.* Moscow: Foreign Language Publishing House, *ca.* 1950.

Payant, Felix (ed.). *A Book of Puppetry.* Columbus, Ohio: Design Publishing Co., 1936.

Poncet, Marie-Thérèse. *L'Esthétique du Dessin Animé.* Paris: Librarie Nezet, 1952.

Poncet, Marie-Thérèse. *Dessin Animé Art Mondial.* Paris: Cercle du Livre, 1956.

Schmidt, Georg; Schmalengach, Werner; and Bächlin, Peter. *The Film, Its Economic, Social, and Artistic Problems,* Eng. ed. London: The Falcon Press, 1948.

Starr, Cecile (ed.). *Ideas on Film.* New York: Funk and Wagnalls, 1951.

Stephenson, Ralph. *Animation in the Cinema.* London: A. Zwemmer, 1967; new and revised edition, Tantivy, 1973.

Tenčík, František. *Hermína Týrlová.* Brno: Krajské Nakladatelství, 1964.

Vánová, Libuše (ed.). *Karel Zeman.* Prague: Československý Filmexport, 1968.

Wollen, Peter. *Signs and Meaning in the Cinema.* Bloomington and London: Indiana University Press, 1969.

Writer's Program of the Works Projects Administration. *The Film Index: A Bibliography, Vol. 1, The Film as Art.* New York: Museum of Modern Art Film Library, and W. H. Wilson Co., 1941.

Youngblood, Gene. *Expanded Cinema.* New York: E. P. Dutton, 1970.

Zanotto, Piero. *Desegni e Pupazzi Animati di Ieri e di Oggi.* Rome: Arti Grafiche Scalia,

Articles

Barker, Felix. "Class-War among the Lilliputians: Ptushko Revises Swift," *World Film News,* December, 1936.

Bond, Kirk. "Formal Cinema," *The New Republic,* June, 1932 (Reprinted in *An Introduction to the Art of the Movies.* Lewis Jacobs (ed.). New York: The Noonday Press, 1960.).

Bray, John Randolph. "Development of Animated Cartoons," *Moving Picture World,* July 21, 1917.

Brenon, Aileen St. John. "Three Thousand Puppets in Motion Pictures," *Design Magazine* (Reprinted in *A Book of Puppetry.* Felix Payant (ed.). Columbus, Ohio: Design Publishing Co., 1936.).

"Colour Puppets Perform Horlick Miracles," *World Film News,* August, 1937.

"Dolls in Motion: Starevitch Reveals Secrets," *World Film News,* April, 1936.

"Emile Cohl, Inventeur des Dessins Animés," *Revue des Deux Mondes,* March 15, 1938.

Hutchins, Patricia. "A Clay Blue-Beard: A New French Puppet Film," *Sight and Sound,* vol. 7, no. 26 (1938).

Hutchins, Patricia. "Puppets on Parade," *Sight and Sound,* vol. 5, no. 19 (1936).

"Hungarian Director [George Pal] Caricatures Celebrities in Colour Cartoons," *World Film News,* June, 1936.

"Jean Gros' Motion Picture Marionettes," *Theater Guild Magazine,* March, 1931.

"Motion Picture Comedies in Clay," *Scientific American,* 115:553, December 16, 1916.

Moulton, Robert H. "Toyland in the Films," *Scientific American,* Vol. 117, No. 26 (December 29, 1917).

Potamkin, Harry. "Ladislas Starevitch and His Doll Films," *Theater Guild Magazine,* December, 1929.

Preduţ, Maria. "Animafilm: Love, Satire, and Suspense," *Romania Today,* June, 1968.

Ptushko, Alexander L. "The Coming of a New Gulliver," *Sight and Sound,* 7:34–5, Summer, 1935.

Richard, A. P. "Emile Cohl," *Technique et Matériel,* December 31, 1937.

Seldes, Gilbert. "Disney and Others," *The New Republic,* June, 1932 (Reprinted in *An Introduction to the Art of the Movies.* Lewis Jacobs (ed.). New York: The Noonday Press, 1960.).

Seton, Marie. "George Pal," *Sight and Sound,* vol. 5, no. 18 (Summer, 1936).

Seton, Marie; "Trick-Film Makers: Starevitch, Reiniger, Bartosch," *World Film News,* October, 1936.

Unpublished Material

Flegler, Joel. *Fact and Fancy: A Study of American Animated Film.* An unpublished monograph for the Annenberg School of Communications, University of Pennsylvania, 1963.

Pojar, Břetislav. "Content of the Speech by Břetislav Pojar." From a typed copy of an address delivered to the Royal Photographic Society, London, 1963.

Above and below: stills from Bretislav Pojar's teddy bear series (photos courtesy of Ceskoslovenský Filmexport).

Index

From THE TALE OF THE FOX *(1929–1939), by Ladislas Starevitch (photo courtesy of the American Film Institute).*